60 Pasta Recipes for Home

By: Kelly Johnson

Table of Contents

Appetizers:

- Classic Spaghetti Bolognese
- Creamy Fettuccine Alfredo
- Penne alla Vodka
- Lemon Garlic Shrimp Linguine
- Pesto Cavatappi with Cherry Tomatoes
- Chicken Carbonara
- Beef and Mushroom Stroganoff
- Spinach and Ricotta Stuffed Shells
- Mediterranean Orzo Salad
- Baked Ziti with Sausage and Peppers
- Cajun Chicken Pasta
- Shrimp Scampi Linguine
- Three-Cheese Baked Rigatoni
- Roasted Red Pepper and Tomato Penne
- Garlic Butter Shrimp and Broccoli Alfredo
- Creamy Tomato Basil Tortellini
- Mushroom and Spinach Lasagna
- Lemon Asparagus Pasta Primavera
- Cajun Seafood Pasta
- Rigatoni with Eggplant and Ricotta
- Beef and Spinach Cannelloni
- Pesto Chicken Caprese Pasta
- Lobster Mac and Cheese
- Mediterranean Lemon Chicken Orzo
- Creamy Sundried Tomato Pappardelle
- Spicy Sausage and Peppers Penne
- Shrimp and Spinach Ravioli in Tomato Cream Sauce
- Mushroom and Goat Cheese Farfalle
- Chicken Marsala Fettuccine
- Creamy Garlic Parmesan Orzo
- Baked Spinach and Artichoke Pasta
- Butternut Squash and Sage Ravioli
- Creamy Cajun Shrimp Linguine

- Caprese Stuffed Portobello Mushroom Pasta
- Chicken and Broccoli Alfredo
- Brown Butter and Sage Gnocchi
- Tomato and Basil Pesto Spaghetti
- Smoky Bacon Carbonara
- Chicken and Mushroom Farfalle
- Creamy Lemon and Asparagus Tagliatelle
- Pumpkin Sage Alfredo with Orecchiette
- Seafood Fra Diavolo Linguine
- Spinach and Feta Stuffed Shells
- Creamy Chipotle Chicken Penne
- Roasted Vegetable and Goat Cheese Lasagna
- Lemon Garlic Butter Shrimp Linguine
- Sundried Tomato and Basil Pesto Cavatelli
- Beef and Spinach Stuffed Shells
- Mushroom and Thyme Tagliatelle
- Mediterranean Chickpea Pasta Salad
- Creamy Bacon and Pea Farfalle
- Chicken and Broccolini Orecchiette
- Sun-Dried Tomato and Artichoke Pesto Rigatoni
- Spicy Sausage and Kale Penne
- Lemon Ricotta Stuffed Shells with Spinach
- Butternut Squash and Bacon Gnocchi
- Creamy Garlic Parmesan Spaghetti
- Shrimp and Avocado Pesto Linguine
- Chicken Piccata with Angel Hair Pasta
- Sweet Potato and Sage Ravioli in Brown Butter Sauce

Classic Spaghetti Bolognese

Ingredients:

- 1 pound (450g) ground beef
- 1 tablespoon olive oil
- 1 onion, finely chopped
- 2 carrots, peeled and diced
- 2 celery stalks, diced
- 3 garlic cloves, minced
- 1/2 cup (120ml) red wine (optional)
- 1 can (28 ounces/800g) crushed tomatoes
- 2 tablespoons tomato paste
- 1 teaspoon dried oregano
- 1 teaspoon dried basil
- 1/2 teaspoon dried thyme
- Salt and pepper to taste
- 1 cup (240ml) beef or vegetable broth
- 1/2 cup (120ml) whole milk or heavy cream
- 1 pound (450g) spaghetti
- Grated Parmesan cheese for serving
- Fresh basil or parsley for garnish (optional)

Instructions:

Heat the olive oil in a large skillet or Dutch oven over medium heat. Add the ground beef and cook until browned, breaking it apart with a spoon as it cooks. Remove any excess fat.

Add the chopped onions, carrots, celery, and minced garlic to the skillet. Cook for about 5 minutes, or until the vegetables are softened.

Pour in the red wine (if using) and cook for 2-3 minutes, allowing it to reduce slightly.

Stir in the crushed tomatoes, tomato paste, dried oregano, dried basil, dried thyme, salt, and pepper. Mix well to combine.

Pour in the beef or vegetable broth and bring the mixture to a simmer. Reduce the heat to low, cover, and let it simmer for at least 1 hour, stirring occasionally. The longer it simmers, the more flavorful it will be.

About 10 minutes before serving, add the whole milk or heavy cream to the sauce, stirring to combine. Adjust the seasoning if needed.

While the sauce is simmering, cook the spaghetti according to the package instructions. Drain and set aside.

Serve the Bolognese sauce over the cooked spaghetti. Garnish with grated Parmesan cheese and fresh basil or parsley if desired.

Enjoy this classic spaghetti Bolognese with a side of crusty bread or a simple green salad. Buon appetito!

Creamy Fettuccine Alfredo

Ingredients:

- 1 pound (450g) fettuccine pasta
- 1/2 cup (1 stick or 113g) unsalted butter
- 2 cups (480ml) heavy cream
- 2 cups (about 200g) freshly grated Parmesan cheese
- Salt and black pepper to taste
- Fresh parsley, chopped, for garnish (optional)

Instructions:

Cook the fettuccine pasta according to the package instructions in a large pot of salted boiling water. Drain and set aside.
In a large skillet or saucepan, melt the butter over medium heat.
Pour in the heavy cream, stirring continuously to combine with the melted butter. Allow the mixture to heat but avoid boiling.
Gradually add the freshly grated Parmesan cheese to the cream and butter mixture, stirring constantly. Continue stirring until the cheese is melted and the sauce becomes smooth and creamy.
Season the Alfredo sauce with salt and black pepper to taste. Be cautious with the salt, as Parmesan is naturally salty.
Add the cooked fettuccine to the skillet or saucepan, tossing it in the creamy Alfredo sauce until the pasta is well-coated.
Continue to cook for an additional 2-3 minutes, allowing the pasta to absorb some of the sauce and heat through.
Serve the creamy fettuccine Alfredo immediately, garnishing with chopped fresh parsley if desired.

Enjoy this indulgent and classic pasta dish! Pair it with a side of garlic bread or a simple green salad for a complete meal. Buon appetito!

Penne alla Vodka

Ingredients:

- 1 pound (450g) penne pasta
- 2 tablespoons olive oil
- 1 small onion, finely chopped
- 2 cloves garlic, minced
- 1/2 teaspoon red pepper flakes (adjust to taste)
- 1 cup (240ml) vodka
- 1 can (28 ounces/800g) crushed tomatoes
- 1 cup (240ml) heavy cream
- Salt and black pepper to taste
- 1/2 cup (50g) grated Parmesan cheese, plus extra for serving
- Fresh basil or parsley, chopped, for garnish

Instructions:

Cook the penne pasta according to the package instructions in a large pot of salted boiling water. Drain and set aside.

In a large skillet, heat the olive oil over medium heat. Add the chopped onion and cook until it becomes translucent, about 3-4 minutes.

Add the minced garlic and red pepper flakes to the skillet, and sauté for an additional 1-2 minutes until fragrant.

Pour in the vodka and let it simmer for 5 minutes, allowing it to reduce by half.

Add the crushed tomatoes to the skillet, stirring to combine with the onion and garlic mixture.

Reduce the heat to low and stir in the heavy cream. Simmer the sauce for about 10-15 minutes, allowing it to thicken.

Season the sauce with salt and black pepper to taste.

Stir in the grated Parmesan cheese, allowing it to melt and further thicken the sauce.

Add the cooked penne to the skillet, tossing to coat the pasta evenly with the vodka-infused tomato cream sauce.

Serve the Penne alla Vodka immediately, garnishing with extra Parmesan cheese and chopped fresh basil or parsley.

Enjoy this rich and flavorful pasta dish with a side of crusty bread or a green salad. Buon appetito!

Lemon Garlic Shrimp Linguine

Ingredients:

- 8 ounces (225g) linguine pasta
- 1 pound (450g) large shrimp, peeled and deveined
- 3 tablespoons olive oil
- 4 cloves garlic, minced
- 1/2 teaspoon red pepper flakes (optional, for heat)
- Zest of 1 lemon
- Juice of 1 lemon
- 1/2 cup (120ml) chicken or vegetable broth
- Salt and black pepper to taste
- 1/4 cup (60ml) dry white wine (optional)
- 1/4 cup (60ml) heavy cream
- 1/4 cup (30g) grated Parmesan cheese
- Fresh parsley, chopped, for garnish

Instructions:

Cook the linguine pasta according to the package instructions in a large pot of salted boiling water. Drain and set aside.
In a large skillet, heat 2 tablespoons of olive oil over medium heat.
Add the shrimp to the skillet and cook for 2-3 minutes per side, or until they are opaque and cooked through. Remove the shrimp from the skillet and set them aside.
In the same skillet, add the remaining 1 tablespoon of olive oil. Sauté the minced garlic and red pepper flakes (if using) for about 1-2 minutes until fragrant.
Pour in the chicken or vegetable broth, scraping the bottom of the skillet to deglaze it.
Add the lemon zest, lemon juice, salt, and black pepper to the skillet. If using white wine, pour it in at this stage. Allow the mixture to simmer for 2-3 minutes.
Reduce the heat to low, stir in the heavy cream, and let it simmer for an additional 2-3 minutes.
Stir in the grated Parmesan cheese until the sauce is smooth and creamy.
Add the cooked linguine to the skillet, tossing to coat the pasta in the lemon garlic cream sauce.

Return the cooked shrimp to the skillet, tossing to combine with the pasta and sauce.
Garnish with fresh parsley and serve the Lemon Garlic Shrimp Linguine immediately.

Enjoy this delightful and zesty shrimp linguine! Pair it with a side of garlic bread or a simple green salad for a complete meal. Buon appetito!

Pesto Cavatappi with Cherry Tomatoes

Ingredients:

- 8 ounces (225g) cavatappi pasta
- 1 cup (about 100g) fresh basil leaves, packed
- 1/2 cup (60g) grated Parmesan cheese
- 1/3 cup (40g) pine nuts, toasted
- 2 cloves garlic, minced
- 1/2 cup (120ml) extra-virgin olive oil
- Salt and black pepper to taste
- 1 pint (about 2 cups or 300g) cherry tomatoes, halved
- 1/2 cup (60g) freshly grated Pecorino Romano cheese
- Fresh basil, chopped, for garnish

Instructions:

Cook the cavatappi pasta according to the package instructions in a large pot of salted boiling water. Drain and set aside.

In a food processor, combine the fresh basil, Parmesan cheese, toasted pine nuts, and minced garlic. Pulse until finely chopped.

With the food processor running, slowly drizzle in the olive oil until the pesto reaches a smooth consistency. Season with salt and black pepper to taste.

In a large mixing bowl, toss the cooked cavatappi pasta with the pesto sauce until evenly coated.

Gently fold in the halved cherry tomatoes, ensuring they are distributed throughout the pasta.

Sprinkle freshly grated Pecorino Romano cheese over the pasta and toss once more.

Garnish the Pesto Cavatappi with chopped fresh basil.

Serve immediately, either warm or at room temperature.

Enjoy this vibrant and flavorful Pesto Cavatappi with Cherry Tomatoes as a light and satisfying meal. It pairs well with a side salad or can be enjoyed on its own. Buon appetito!

Chicken Carbonara

Ingredients:

- 8 ounces (225g) spaghetti
- 1 tablespoon olive oil
- 1 pound (450g) boneless, skinless chicken breasts, thinly sliced
- Salt and black pepper to taste
- 4 slices of bacon, chopped
- 3 cloves garlic, minced
- 3 large eggs
- 1 cup (about 100g) grated Parmesan cheese
- 1/2 cup (120ml) heavy cream
- Fresh parsley, chopped, for garnish

Instructions:

Cook the spaghetti according to the package instructions in a large pot of salted boiling water. Drain and set aside.
Season the sliced chicken breasts with salt and black pepper.
In a large skillet, heat the olive oil over medium-high heat. Add the seasoned chicken slices and cook until browned and cooked through, about 5-7 minutes. Remove the chicken from the skillet and set it aside.
In the same skillet, add the chopped bacon and cook until crispy. Add minced garlic and sauté for about 1 minute until fragrant.
In a bowl, whisk together the eggs, grated Parmesan cheese, and heavy cream.
Add the cooked spaghetti to the skillet with bacon and garlic. Toss to coat the pasta in the bacon fat.
Remove the skillet from heat, and quickly pour the egg and cheese mixture over the spaghetti, tossing continuously to coat the pasta and create a creamy sauce. Be careful not to scramble the eggs; the heat from the pasta will cook them gently.
Return the cooked chicken to the skillet, tossing with the pasta until well combined.
Season with additional salt and black pepper if needed.
Garnish the Chicken Carbonara with chopped fresh parsley and serve immediately.

Enjoy this comforting and creamy Chicken Carbonara as a hearty meal. Serve it with a side of garlic bread or a simple salad for a complete dining experience. Buon appetito!

Beef and Mushroom Stroganoff

Ingredients:

- 1 pound (450g) beef sirloin or tenderloin, thinly sliced
- Salt and black pepper to taste
- 2 tablespoons olive oil
- 1 onion, finely chopped
- 2 cloves garlic, minced
- 8 ounces (225g) cremini or button mushrooms, sliced
- 2 tablespoons all-purpose flour
- 1 cup (240ml) beef broth
- 2 tablespoons Worcestershire sauce
- 1 tablespoon Dijon mustard
- 1/2 cup (120ml) sour cream
- 8 ounces (225g) egg noodles or your preferred pasta
- Fresh parsley, chopped, for garnish

Instructions:

Season the thinly sliced beef with salt and black pepper.
Heat olive oil in a large skillet over medium-high heat. Add the sliced beef and cook until browned on all sides. Remove the beef from the skillet and set it aside.
In the same skillet, add chopped onions and cook until they become translucent, about 3-4 minutes.
Add minced garlic and sliced mushrooms to the skillet. Sauté until the mushrooms are tender and any released moisture evaporates.
Sprinkle flour over the mushroom mixture and stir well to coat.
Gradually pour in the beef broth, Worcestershire sauce, and Dijon mustard, stirring continuously to create a smooth sauce.
Bring the mixture to a simmer and let it cook for a few minutes until it thickens.
Reduce the heat to low, return the cooked beef to the skillet, and simmer for an additional 5-7 minutes, allowing the flavors to meld.
Meanwhile, cook the egg noodles or pasta according to the package instructions in a large pot of salted boiling water. Drain and set aside.
Just before serving, stir in the sour cream into the beef and mushroom mixture, heating through without boiling.
Season the stroganoff with additional salt and black pepper to taste.
Serve the Beef and Mushroom Stroganoff over the cooked noodles or pasta.

Garnish with chopped fresh parsley.

Enjoy this comforting and flavorful Beef and Mushroom Stroganoff for a satisfying meal. Pair it with a side of steamed vegetables or a green salad. Bon appétit!

Spinach and Ricotta Stuffed Shells

Ingredients:

- 1 box (12 ounces or 340g) jumbo pasta shells
- 2 cups (500g) ricotta cheese
- 1 cup (100g) grated Parmesan cheese
- 1 egg, lightly beaten
- 1 cup (90g) chopped fresh spinach, cooked and drained
- 1 teaspoon dried oregano
- 1 teaspoon dried basil
- 1/2 teaspoon garlic powder
- Salt and black pepper to taste
- 2 cups (480ml) marinara sauce
- 1 cup (100g) shredded mozzarella cheese
- Fresh basil or parsley, chopped, for garnish

Instructions:

Cook the jumbo pasta shells according to the package instructions in a large pot of salted boiling water. Drain and set aside.
Preheat the oven to 375°F (190°C).
In a mixing bowl, combine the ricotta cheese, grated Parmesan cheese, beaten egg, chopped spinach, dried oregano, dried basil, garlic powder, salt, and black pepper. Mix well until all ingredients are evenly incorporated.
Spoon the spinach and ricotta mixture into the cooked jumbo pasta shells, filling each shell generously.
Spread a thin layer of marinara sauce on the bottom of a baking dish.
Arrange the stuffed shells in the baking dish, placing them close together.
Pour the remaining marinara sauce over the stuffed shells, covering them evenly.
Sprinkle shredded mozzarella cheese over the top of the shells.
Cover the baking dish with aluminum foil and bake in the preheated oven for 25-30 minutes, or until the cheese is melted and bubbly.
Remove the foil and bake for an additional 5-10 minutes, or until the cheese is golden and slightly crispy.
Garnish with chopped fresh basil or parsley before serving.
Allow the stuffed shells to cool slightly before serving.

Enjoy these delicious Spinach and Ricotta Stuffed Shells as a comforting and flavorful main dish. Serve with a side salad or garlic bread for a complete meal. Buon appetito!

Mediterranean Orzo Salad

Ingredients:

- 1 cup (200g) orzo pasta
- 2 cups (470ml) vegetable broth or water
- 1 cup (150g) cherry tomatoes, halved
- 1 cucumber, diced
- 1/2 red bell pepper, diced
- 1/2 yellow bell pepper, diced
- 1/4 cup (40g) red onion, finely chopped
- 1/2 cup (80g) Kalamata olives, pitted and sliced
- 1/2 cup (75g) crumbled feta cheese
- 1/4 cup (30g) fresh parsley, chopped
- 1/4 cup (60ml) extra-virgin olive oil
- 2 tablespoons red wine vinegar
- 1 teaspoon dried oregano
- Salt and black pepper to taste
- Lemon wedges for serving (optional)

Instructions:

Cook the orzo pasta in vegetable broth or water according to the package instructions until al dente. Drain and let it cool to room temperature.
In a large mixing bowl, combine the cooked orzo, cherry tomatoes, diced cucumber, diced red and yellow bell peppers, chopped red onion, sliced Kalamata olives, crumbled feta cheese, and chopped fresh parsley.
In a small bowl, whisk together the extra-virgin olive oil, red wine vinegar, dried oregano, salt, and black pepper to create the dressing.
Pour the dressing over the orzo mixture and toss gently to coat everything evenly. Adjust the seasoning if needed, adding more salt, pepper, or olive oil to taste.
Chill the Mediterranean Orzo Salad in the refrigerator for at least 1 hour to allow the flavors to meld.
Before serving, give the salad a final gentle toss and garnish with additional fresh parsley.
Serve the salad cold, optionally with lemon wedges on the side for an extra burst of freshness.

Enjoy this vibrant and flavorful Mediterranean Orzo Salad as a light and refreshing side dish or a standalone meal. It's perfect for picnics, barbecues, or as a healthy lunch option. Bon appétit!

Baked Ziti with Sausage and Peppers

Ingredients:

- 1 pound (450g) ziti pasta
- 1 tablespoon olive oil
- 1 pound (450g) Italian sausage, casings removed
- 1 onion, sliced
- 1 red bell pepper, sliced
- 1 yellow bell pepper, sliced
- 3 cloves garlic, minced
- 1 can (28 ounces/800g) crushed tomatoes
- 1 teaspoon dried oregano
- 1 teaspoon dried basil
- Salt and black pepper to taste
- 2 cups (200g) shredded mozzarella cheese
- 1/2 cup (50g) grated Parmesan cheese
- Fresh basil or parsley, chopped, for garnish

Instructions:

Preheat the oven to 375°F (190°C).
Cook the ziti pasta according to the package instructions in a large pot of salted boiling water. Drain and set aside.
In a large skillet, heat olive oil over medium heat. Add the Italian sausage, breaking it apart with a spoon, and cook until browned. Remove any excess fat.
Add sliced onions and bell peppers to the skillet. Sauté until the vegetables are softened.
Stir in minced garlic and cook for an additional 1-2 minutes until fragrant.
Pour in the crushed tomatoes, dried oregano, dried basil, salt, and black pepper. Mix well and let it simmer for about 10 minutes, allowing the flavors to meld.
In a large mixing bowl, combine the cooked ziti with the sausage and peppers mixture. Mix until the pasta is evenly coated with the sauce.
In a greased baking dish, layer half of the ziti mixture, followed by half of the shredded mozzarella and Parmesan cheese. Repeat with the remaining ziti mixture and cheeses.
Bake in the preheated oven for 20-25 minutes, or until the cheese is melted and bubbly, and the edges are golden brown.
Garnish with chopped fresh basil or parsley before serving.

Allow the Baked Ziti with Sausage and Peppers to cool slightly before serving.

Enjoy this hearty and flavorful baked pasta dish as a comforting family dinner. Serve with a side salad or garlic bread for a complete meal. Buon appetito!

Cajun Chicken Pasta

Ingredients:

- 8 ounces (225g) linguine or fettuccine pasta
- 2 boneless, skinless chicken breasts, thinly sliced
- 2 tablespoons Cajun seasoning
- 2 tablespoons olive oil
- 1 tablespoon butter
- 1 red bell pepper, thinly sliced
- 1 green bell pepper, thinly sliced
- 1 small red onion, thinly sliced
- 3 cloves garlic, minced
- 1 cup (240ml) chicken broth
- 1 cup (240ml) heavy cream
- 1/2 cup (50g) grated Parmesan cheese
- Salt and black pepper to taste
- Fresh parsley, chopped, for garnish

Instructions:

Cook the linguine or fettuccine pasta according to the package instructions in a large pot of salted boiling water. Drain and set aside.

In a bowl, toss the thinly sliced chicken breasts with Cajun seasoning until well coated.

Heat olive oil in a large skillet over medium-high heat. Add the Cajun-seasoned chicken slices and cook until browned and cooked through. Remove the chicken from the skillet and set it aside.

In the same skillet, add butter and sauté the sliced red and green bell peppers, and red onion until softened.

Add minced garlic to the skillet and sauté for an additional 1-2 minutes until fragrant.

Pour in the chicken broth and bring it to a simmer. Allow it to cook for a couple of minutes to reduce slightly.

Reduce the heat to low, stir in the heavy cream, and let it simmer for another 2-3 minutes.

Stir in the grated Parmesan cheese until the sauce is smooth and creamy.

Return the cooked Cajun chicken to the skillet, tossing it in the creamy sauce to coat.

Season the sauce with salt and black pepper to taste.
Add the cooked pasta to the skillet, tossing until the pasta is well-coated in the Cajun chicken and creamy sauce.
Serve the Cajun Chicken Pasta hot, garnished with chopped fresh parsley.

Enjoy this spicy and flavorful Cajun Chicken Pasta for a satisfying meal. Serve with a side of garlic bread or a simple green salad. Bon appétit!

Shrimp Scampi Linguine

Ingredients:

- 8 ounces (225g) linguine pasta
- 1 pound (450g) large shrimp, peeled and deveined
- Salt and black pepper to taste
- 3 tablespoons unsalted butter
- 3 tablespoons olive oil
- 4 cloves garlic, minced
- 1/2 teaspoon red pepper flakes (adjust to taste)
- Zest of 1 lemon
- Juice of 1 lemon
- 1/2 cup (120ml) dry white wine
- 1/2 cup (120ml) chicken or vegetable broth
- 1/4 cup (60ml) fresh lemon juice
- 1/4 cup (60ml) chopped fresh parsley
- Grated Parmesan cheese for serving (optional)

Instructions:

Cook the linguine pasta according to the package instructions in a large pot of salted boiling water. Drain and set aside.
Season the shrimp with salt and black pepper.
In a large skillet, heat 2 tablespoons of butter and 2 tablespoons of olive oil over medium-high heat.
Add the seasoned shrimp to the skillet and cook for 1-2 minutes per side, or until they turn pink and opaque. Remove the shrimp from the skillet and set them aside.
In the same skillet, add the remaining 1 tablespoon of butter and 1 tablespoon of olive oil.
Sauté the minced garlic and red pepper flakes (if using) for about 1-2 minutes until fragrant.
Pour in the dry white wine, chicken or vegetable broth, and fresh lemon juice.
Bring the mixture to a simmer, scraping any browned bits from the bottom of the skillet.
Reduce the heat to low, return the cooked shrimp to the skillet, and toss them in the sauce.

Add the cooked linguine to the skillet, tossing to coat the pasta in the flavorful shrimp scampi sauce.
Sprinkle chopped fresh parsley over the dish and toss once more.
Serve the Shrimp Scampi Linguine immediately, optionally garnishing with grated Parmesan cheese.

Enjoy this delicious and zesty Shrimp Scampi Linguine for a light and flavorful meal. Pair it with a side of crusty bread or a simple green salad. Buon appetito!

Three-Cheese Baked Rigatoni

Ingredients:

- 1 pound (450g) rigatoni pasta
- 2 tablespoons olive oil
- 1 onion, finely chopped
- 3 cloves garlic, minced
- 1 can (28 ounces/800g) crushed tomatoes
- 1 teaspoon dried oregano
- 1 teaspoon dried basil
- Salt and black pepper to taste
- 1 cup (240ml) ricotta cheese
- 1 cup (100g) grated Parmesan cheese
- 1 cup (120g) shredded mozzarella cheese
- 1/4 cup (60ml) heavy cream
- Fresh basil or parsley, chopped, for garnish

Instructions:

Preheat the oven to 375°F (190°C).
Cook the rigatoni pasta according to the package instructions in a large pot of salted boiling water. Drain and set aside.
In a large skillet, heat olive oil over medium heat. Add the chopped onion and sauté until it becomes translucent.
Add minced garlic to the skillet and cook for an additional 1-2 minutes until fragrant.
Pour in the crushed tomatoes, dried oregano, dried basil, salt, and black pepper. Mix well and let it simmer for about 10-15 minutes, allowing the sauce to thicken.
In a large mixing bowl, combine the cooked rigatoni with the tomato sauce, tossing to coat the pasta evenly.
In a separate bowl, mix together the ricotta cheese, grated Parmesan cheese, shredded mozzarella cheese, and heavy cream until well combined.
In a greased baking dish, layer half of the rigatoni and tomato sauce mixture. Top it with half of the three-cheese mixture. Repeat the layers.
Bake in the preheated oven for 20-25 minutes, or until the cheese is melted and bubbly, and the edges are golden brown.
Garnish with chopped fresh basil or parsley before serving.

Allow the Three-Cheese Baked Rigatoni to cool slightly before serving.

Enjoy this comforting and cheesy baked pasta dish as a hearty family dinner. Serve with a side salad or garlic bread for a complete meal. Buon appetito!

Roasted Red Pepper and Tomato Penne

Ingredients:

- 12 ounces (340g) penne pasta
- 2 large red bell peppers
- 1 can (28 ounces/800g) whole peeled tomatoes
- 3 tablespoons olive oil
- 1 onion, finely chopped
- 3 cloves garlic, minced
- 1 teaspoon dried oregano
- 1 teaspoon dried basil
- Salt and black pepper to taste
- 1/2 teaspoon red pepper flakes (optional, for heat)
- 1/2 cup (120ml) heavy cream
- 1/4 cup (30g) grated Parmesan cheese
- Fresh basil, chopped, for garnish

Instructions:

Preheat the oven to 400°F (200°C).
Place the red bell peppers on a baking sheet and roast them in the preheated oven for 20-25 minutes, turning occasionally, until the skin is charred and blistered. Remove from the oven and let them cool slightly. Once cooled, peel off the skin, remove the seeds, and chop the roasted peppers.
In a blender or food processor, puree the whole peeled tomatoes until smooth.
Cook the penne pasta according to the package instructions in a large pot of salted boiling water. Drain and set aside.
In a large skillet, heat olive oil over medium heat. Add the chopped onion and sauté until it becomes translucent.
Add minced garlic to the skillet and cook for an additional 1-2 minutes until fragrant.
Stir in the chopped roasted red peppers, tomato puree, dried oregano, dried basil, salt, black pepper, and red pepper flakes (if using). Let the sauce simmer for 10-15 minutes, allowing the flavors to meld.
Reduce the heat to low, stir in the heavy cream, and let it simmer for an additional 2-3 minutes.

Add the cooked penne to the skillet, tossing to coat the pasta in the roasted red pepper and tomato sauce.
Stir in the grated Parmesan cheese until the sauce is creamy and well combined.
Garnish the Roasted Red Pepper and Tomato Penne with chopped fresh basil.
Serve immediately, optionally with extra Parmesan cheese on the side.

Enjoy this flavorful and vibrant Roasted Red Pepper and Tomato Penne as a delicious and satisfying meal. Pair it with a side salad or garlic bread for a complete dining experience. Buon appetito!

Garlic Butter Shrimp and Broccoli Alfredo

Ingredients:

- 8 ounces (225g) fettuccine or linguine pasta
- 1 pound (450g) large shrimp, peeled and deveined
- Salt and black pepper to taste
- 3 tablespoons unsalted butter
- 4 cloves garlic, minced
- 1 cup (240ml) chicken broth
- 1 cup (240ml) heavy cream
- 1 cup (100g) grated Parmesan cheese
- 1 cup (150g) broccoli florets, blanched
- 1 teaspoon dried parsley (or fresh parsley for garnish)
- Lemon wedges for serving (optional)

Instructions:

Cook the fettuccine or linguine pasta according to the package instructions in a large pot of salted boiling water. Drain and set aside.
Season the shrimp with salt and black pepper.
In a large skillet, melt 2 tablespoons of butter over medium-high heat. Add the seasoned shrimp and cook for 1-2 minutes per side, or until they turn pink and opaque. Remove the shrimp from the skillet and set them aside.
In the same skillet, add the remaining 1 tablespoon of butter. Sauté minced garlic until fragrant, about 1-2 minutes.
Pour in the chicken broth, scraping any browned bits from the bottom of the skillet. Let it simmer for 2-3 minutes.
Reduce the heat to low, pour in the heavy cream, and simmer for an additional 2-3 minutes.
Stir in the grated Parmesan cheese until the sauce is smooth and creamy.
Add the blanched broccoli florets and cooked shrimp to the skillet, tossing to coat them in the garlic butter Alfredo sauce.
Season the sauce with dried parsley and adjust the salt and pepper to taste.
Add the cooked pasta to the skillet, tossing until the pasta is well-coated in the creamy sauce and mixed with shrimp and broccoli.
Serve the Garlic Butter Shrimp and Broccoli Alfredo immediately, optionally garnishing with fresh parsley and lemon wedges.

Enjoy this indulgent and flavorful pasta dish! Pair it with a side of garlic bread or a green salad for a complete meal. Buon appetito!

Creamy Tomato Basil Tortellini

Ingredients:

- 1 pound (450g) cheese tortellini
- 2 tablespoons olive oil
- 1 small onion, finely chopped
- 3 cloves garlic, minced
- 1 can (28 ounces/800g) crushed tomatoes
- 1 teaspoon dried basil
- 1/2 teaspoon dried oregano
- Salt and black pepper to taste
- 1 cup (240ml) heavy cream
- 1/2 cup (50g) grated Parmesan cheese
- 1/4 cup (60ml) fresh basil, chopped, plus extra for garnish
- 1/4 teaspoon red pepper flakes (optional, for heat)
- Grated Parmesan or shredded mozzarella for serving (optional)

Instructions:

Cook the cheese tortellini according to the package instructions in a large pot of salted boiling water. Drain and set aside.
In a large skillet, heat olive oil over medium heat. Add the chopped onion and sauté until it becomes translucent.
Add minced garlic to the skillet and cook for an additional 1-2 minutes until fragrant.
Pour in the crushed tomatoes, dried basil, dried oregano, salt, and black pepper. Stir well and let it simmer for about 10 minutes, allowing the flavors to meld.
Reduce the heat to low, pour in the heavy cream, and simmer for an additional 2-3 minutes.
Stir in the grated Parmesan cheese until the sauce is smooth and creamy.
Add the cooked tortellini to the skillet, tossing to coat the pasta in the creamy tomato basil sauce.
Add chopped fresh basil and red pepper flakes (if using), tossing once more.
Adjust the seasoning if needed and serve the Creamy Tomato Basil Tortellini hot. Garnish with extra fresh basil and grated Parmesan or shredded mozzarella, if desired.

Enjoy this luscious and comforting Creamy Tomato Basil Tortellini as a delightful and satisfying meal. Pair it with a side salad or garlic bread for a complete dining experience. Buon appetito!

Mushroom and Spinach Lasagna

Ingredients:

- 9 lasagna noodles, cooked according to package instructions
- 2 tablespoons olive oil
- 1 onion, finely chopped
- 3 cloves garlic, minced
- 8 ounces (225g) cremini or white mushrooms, sliced
- 6 cups (about 180g) fresh spinach, chopped
- 1 can (28 ounces/800g) crushed tomatoes
- 1 teaspoon dried oregano
- 1 teaspoon dried basil
- Salt and black pepper to taste
- 15 ounces (425g) ricotta cheese
- 1 egg, beaten
- 2 cups (200g) shredded mozzarella cheese
- 1/2 cup (50g) grated Parmesan cheese
- Fresh basil or parsley, chopped, for garnish

Instructions:

Preheat the oven to 375°F (190°C).
In a large skillet, heat olive oil over medium heat. Add the chopped onion and sauté until it becomes translucent.
Add minced garlic to the skillet and cook for an additional 1-2 minutes until fragrant.
Add sliced mushrooms to the skillet and cook until they release their moisture and become tender.
Stir in the chopped fresh spinach and cook until wilted. Season with salt and black pepper.
Pour in the crushed tomatoes, dried oregano, dried basil, and let the mixture simmer for about 10-15 minutes. Adjust the seasoning if needed.
In a bowl, combine the ricotta cheese with the beaten egg, mixing well.
In a greased baking dish, spread a thin layer of the tomato and mushroom mixture.
Place a layer of cooked lasagna noodles over the sauce.

Spread half of the ricotta mixture over the noodles, followed by a layer of the tomato and mushroom mixture. Sprinkle with mozzarella and Parmesan cheese. Repeat the layers, finishing with a layer of tomato and mushroom mixture and a generous topping of mozzarella and Parmesan cheese.

Cover the baking dish with aluminum foil and bake in the preheated oven for 25-30 minutes.

Remove the foil and bake for an additional 10-15 minutes, or until the cheese is golden and bubbly.

Let the Mushroom and Spinach Lasagna rest for a few minutes before slicing. Garnish with chopped fresh basil or parsley before serving.

Enjoy this delicious and hearty Mushroom and Spinach Lasagna as a comforting and flavorful meal. Serve with a side salad or garlic bread for a complete dining experience.

Buon appetito!

Lemon Asparagus Pasta Primavera

Ingredients:

- 8 ounces (225g) fettuccine or your favorite pasta
- 1 bunch asparagus, trimmed and cut into bite-sized pieces
- 2 tablespoons olive oil
- 4 cloves garlic, minced
- 1 cup (150g) cherry tomatoes, halved
- 1 bell pepper, thinly sliced
- 1/2 cup (75g) frozen peas, thawed
- Zest of 1 lemon
- Juice of 1 lemon
- 1/4 cup (60ml) vegetable broth or white wine
- Salt and black pepper to taste
- 1/4 cup (30g) grated Parmesan cheese
- Fresh basil or parsley, chopped, for garnish

Instructions:

Cook the fettuccine or pasta according to the package instructions in a large pot of salted boiling water. Drain and set aside.

In a large skillet, heat olive oil over medium heat. Add minced garlic and sauté for about 1-2 minutes until fragrant.

Add the asparagus pieces to the skillet and cook for 3-4 minutes until they are bright green and slightly tender.

Stir in the cherry tomatoes, sliced bell pepper, and thawed peas. Cook for an additional 2-3 minutes, allowing the vegetables to soften.

Pour in the vegetable broth or white wine, lemon zest, and lemon juice. Season with salt and black pepper. Allow the mixture to simmer for 2-3 minutes.

Add the cooked pasta to the skillet, tossing to coat the pasta in the lemony vegetable mixture.

Sprinkle grated Parmesan cheese over the pasta and toss once more until the cheese is melted and incorporated.

Garnish the Lemon Asparagus Pasta Primavera with chopped fresh basil or parsley.

Serve immediately, optionally with additional Parmesan cheese on the side.

Enjoy this vibrant and refreshing Lemon Asparagus Pasta Primavera as a light and flavorful meal. It's perfect for spring and summer days. Buon appetito!

Cajun Seafood Pasta

Ingredients:

- 8 ounces (225g) fettuccine or linguine pasta
- 2 tablespoons olive oil
- 1 pound (450g) shrimp, peeled and deveined
- 1 pound (450g) scallops
- 1 tablespoon Cajun seasoning
- 1 onion, finely chopped
- 3 cloves garlic, minced
- 1 bell pepper, thinly sliced
- 1 cup (240ml) chicken broth
- 1 cup (240ml) heavy cream
- 1 teaspoon dried thyme
- 1 teaspoon dried oregano
- 1/2 teaspoon paprika
- Salt and black pepper to taste
- 1/4 cup (30g) grated Parmesan cheese
- Fresh parsley, chopped, for garnish
- Lemon wedges for serving (optional)

Instructions:

Cook the fettuccine or linguine pasta according to the package instructions in a large pot of salted boiling water. Drain and set aside.
In a large skillet, heat olive oil over medium-high heat. Season the shrimp and scallops with Cajun seasoning.
Add the seasoned shrimp and scallops to the skillet and cook until they are browned and cooked through. Remove them from the skillet and set aside.
In the same skillet, add chopped onion and sauté until it becomes translucent.
Add minced garlic and sliced bell pepper to the skillet. Cook for an additional 2-3 minutes until the bell pepper is tender.
Pour in the chicken broth, heavy cream, dried thyme, dried oregano, paprika, salt, and black pepper. Stir well and let the mixture simmer for about 5 minutes, allowing the flavors to meld.
Return the cooked shrimp and scallops to the skillet, tossing to coat them in the Cajun cream sauce. Let it simmer for an additional 2-3 minutes.

Add the cooked pasta to the skillet, tossing until the pasta is well-coated in the creamy Cajun seafood sauce.
Stir in the grated Parmesan cheese until the sauce is smooth and has a velvety texture.
Garnish the Cajun Seafood Pasta with chopped fresh parsley.
Serve immediately, optionally with lemon wedges on the side for an extra burst of flavor.

Enjoy this spicy and indulgent Cajun Seafood Pasta for a delightful and satisfying meal. Pair it with a side of garlic bread or a simple green salad. Buon appetito!

Rigatoni with Eggplant and Ricotta

Ingredients:

- 1 pound (450g) rigatoni pasta
- 1 medium eggplant, diced
- Salt for sweating the eggplant
- 3 tablespoons olive oil, divided
- 1 onion, finely chopped
- 3 cloves garlic, minced
- 1 can (28 ounces/800g) crushed tomatoes
- 1 teaspoon dried oregano
- 1 teaspoon dried basil
- Red pepper flakes (optional, for heat)
- Salt and black pepper to taste
- 1 cup (240g) ricotta cheese
- 1/2 cup (50g) grated Parmesan cheese
- Fresh basil, chopped, for garnish

Instructions:

Preheat the oven to 400°F (200°C).

Dice the eggplant into small cubes and sprinkle with salt. Allow it to sit for about 20 minutes to draw out excess moisture. Rinse and pat dry with paper towels.

Toss the diced eggplant with 2 tablespoons of olive oil and spread it in a single layer on a baking sheet. Roast in the preheated oven for 20-25 minutes or until golden brown and tender.

Cook the rigatoni pasta according to the package instructions in a large pot of salted boiling water. Drain and set aside.

In a large skillet, heat the remaining 1 tablespoon of olive oil over medium heat. Add the chopped onion and sauté until it becomes translucent.

Add minced garlic to the skillet and cook for an additional 1-2 minutes until fragrant.

Pour in the crushed tomatoes, dried oregano, dried basil, and red pepper flakes (if using). Season with salt and black pepper. Let the mixture simmer for about 10-15 minutes.

Stir in the roasted eggplant cubes and let the flavors meld for an additional 5 minutes.

In a serving bowl, combine the cooked rigatoni with the eggplant and tomato sauce.
Dollop ricotta cheese over the pasta and gently toss to combine.
Sprinkle grated Parmesan cheese over the top and garnish with chopped fresh basil.
Serve the Rigatoni with Eggplant and Ricotta immediately.

Enjoy this flavorful and comforting pasta dish featuring the delicious combination of eggplant and ricotta. It's a perfect meal for a satisfying dinner. Buon appetito!

Beef and Spinach Cannelloni

Ingredients:

For the Filling:

- 1 pound (450g) ground beef
- 1 onion, finely chopped
- 3 cloves garlic, minced
- 1 cup (150g) frozen chopped spinach, thawed and drained
- 1 cup (250g) ricotta cheese
- 1/2 cup (50g) grated Parmesan cheese
- 1 egg, beaten
- Salt and black pepper to taste

For the Sauce:

- 2 tablespoons olive oil
- 1 can (28 ounces/800g) crushed tomatoes
- 1 teaspoon dried oregano
- 1 teaspoon dried basil
- Salt and black pepper to taste

Other Ingredients:

- 1 package (8 ounces/225g) cannelloni tubes
- 1 1/2 cups (150g) shredded mozzarella cheese
- Fresh parsley, chopped, for garnish

Instructions:

Preheat the oven to 375°F (190°C).
In a large skillet, heat olive oil over medium heat. Add chopped onion and sauté until it becomes translucent.
Add minced garlic to the skillet and cook for an additional 1-2 minutes until fragrant.
Add ground beef to the skillet and cook until browned. Drain any excess fat.
In a bowl, combine the cooked ground beef, thawed and drained chopped spinach, ricotta cheese, grated Parmesan cheese, beaten egg, salt, and black pepper. Mix well to create the filling.

In a separate saucepan, heat olive oil over medium heat. Add crushed tomatoes, dried oregano, dried basil, salt, and black pepper. Let the sauce simmer for about 10 minutes.

Fill the cannelloni tubes with the beef and spinach mixture using a spoon or a piping bag.

Pour a thin layer of tomato sauce into the bottom of a baking dish.

Arrange the filled cannelloni tubes in the baking dish.

Pour the remaining tomato sauce over the top of the cannelloni.

Sprinkle shredded mozzarella cheese evenly over the sauce.

Cover the baking dish with aluminum foil and bake in the preheated oven for 25-30 minutes.

Remove the foil and bake for an additional 10-15 minutes, or until the cheese is melted and bubbly, and the edges are golden brown.

Garnish with chopped fresh parsley before serving.

Allow the Beef and Spinach Cannelloni to cool slightly before serving.

Enjoy this hearty and delicious Beef and Spinach Cannelloni as a comforting family dinner. Serve with a side salad or garlic bread for a complete meal. Buon appetito!

Pesto Chicken Caprese Pasta

Ingredients:

- 8 ounces (225g) pasta (penne or your choice)
- 1 pound (450g) boneless, skinless chicken breasts, thinly sliced
- Salt and black pepper to taste
- 2 tablespoons olive oil, divided
- 1/2 cup (120ml) basil pesto (store-bought or homemade)
- 1 cup (150g) cherry tomatoes, halved
- 8 ounces (225g) fresh mozzarella, diced
- Balsamic glaze, for drizzling
- Fresh basil, chopped, for garnish

Instructions:

Cook the pasta according to the package instructions in a large pot of salted boiling water. Drain and set aside.
Season the thinly sliced chicken breasts with salt and black pepper.
In a large skillet, heat 1 tablespoon of olive oil over medium-high heat. Add the seasoned chicken slices and cook until browned and cooked through. Remove from the skillet and set aside.
In the same skillet, add the remaining 1 tablespoon of olive oil. Add the cherry tomatoes and sauté for 2-3 minutes until they are slightly softened.
Add the cooked pasta to the skillet, tossing to combine with the tomatoes.
Stir in the basil pesto, ensuring the pasta and tomatoes are evenly coated.
Add the cooked chicken slices back to the skillet, mixing them with the pasta and pesto.
Toss in the diced fresh mozzarella and cook for an additional 1-2 minutes until the cheese begins to melt.
Season with additional salt and black pepper if needed.
Drizzle balsamic glaze over the Pesto Chicken Caprese Pasta.
Garnish with chopped fresh basil.
Serve immediately, optionally with extra balsamic glaze on the side.

Enjoy this flavorful and vibrant Pesto Chicken Caprese Pasta for a delicious and satisfying meal. It's a perfect combination of fresh and savory flavors. Buon appetito!

Lobster Mac and Cheese

Ingredients:

- 8 ounces (225g) elbow macaroni or your favorite pasta
- 2 lobster tails, cooked and meat removed, chopped into bite-sized pieces
- 1/4 cup (60g) unsalted butter
- 1/4 cup (30g) all-purpose flour
- 2 cups (480ml) whole milk
- 1 cup (240ml) heavy cream
- 2 cups (200g) shredded sharp cheddar cheese
- 1 cup (100g) shredded Gruyère cheese
- 1/2 cup (50g) grated Parmesan cheese
- 1 teaspoon Dijon mustard
- 1/2 teaspoon paprika
- Salt and black pepper to taste
- 1/2 cup (60g) breadcrumbs
- Fresh parsley, chopped, for garnish

Instructions:

Cook the elbow macaroni or pasta according to the package instructions in a large pot of salted boiling water. Drain and set aside.

In a large saucepan, melt the butter over medium heat. Add the flour and whisk continuously to create a roux. Cook for 1-2 minutes until it becomes golden brown.

Gradually pour in the whole milk and heavy cream, whisking constantly to avoid lumps. Continue to whisk until the mixture thickens, about 5-7 minutes.

Reduce the heat to low and add the shredded cheddar, Gruyère, and grated Parmesan cheese to the sauce. Stir until the cheese is melted and the sauce is smooth.

Stir in the Dijon mustard, paprika, salt, and black pepper to taste.

Add the cooked and chopped lobster meat to the cheese sauce, stirring gently to combine.

Preheat the oven to 375°F (190°C).

In a small bowl, mix the breadcrumbs with a tablespoon of melted butter.

Combine the cooked pasta with the lobster and cheese sauce. Transfer the mixture to a greased baking dish.

Sprinkle the breadcrumb mixture evenly over the top of the mac and cheese.

Bake in the preheated oven for 20-25 minutes, or until the top is golden brown and the cheese is bubbly.
Remove from the oven and let it rest for a few minutes before serving.
Garnish with chopped fresh parsley before serving.

Enjoy this luxurious and indulgent Lobster Mac and Cheese for a special meal. It's a perfect blend of creamy cheese sauce and succulent lobster. Buon appetito!

Mediterranean Lemon Chicken Orzo

Ingredients:

- 1 pound (450g) boneless, skinless chicken breasts, cut into bite-sized pieces
- Salt and black pepper to taste
- 2 tablespoons olive oil, divided
- 1 cup (200g) cherry tomatoes, halved
- 1 cup (150g) Kalamata olives, pitted and sliced
- 1 cup (200g) artichoke hearts, quartered
- 1 cup (200g) baby spinach
- 2 cups (400g) cooked orzo pasta
- 3 cloves garlic, minced
- Zest and juice of 1 lemon
- 1 teaspoon dried oregano
- 1/2 teaspoon dried thyme
- 1/2 cup (120ml) chicken broth
- Feta cheese, crumbled, for garnish
- Fresh parsley, chopped, for garnish

Instructions:

Season the chicken pieces with salt and black pepper.
In a large skillet, heat 1 tablespoon of olive oil over medium-high heat. Add the seasoned chicken and cook until browned and cooked through. Remove from the skillet and set aside.
In the same skillet, add the remaining 1 tablespoon of olive oil. Sauté minced garlic until fragrant.
Add cherry tomatoes, Kalamata olives, and artichoke hearts to the skillet. Cook for 2-3 minutes until the tomatoes are slightly softened.
Pour in the chicken broth, lemon zest, lemon juice, dried oregano, and dried thyme. Allow the mixture to simmer for about 2-3 minutes.
Add the cooked orzo pasta, cooked chicken, and baby spinach to the skillet. Toss gently to combine and heat through until the spinach wilts.
Adjust the seasoning with salt and black pepper as needed.
Garnish with crumbled feta cheese and chopped fresh parsley.
Serve the Mediterranean Lemon Chicken Orzo immediately.

Enjoy this vibrant and flavorful Mediterranean Lemon Chicken Orzo for a light and refreshing meal. It's a perfect combination of citrusy flavors, tender chicken, and Mediterranean-inspired ingredients. Buon appetito!

Creamy Sundried Tomato Pappardelle

Ingredients:

- 12 ounces (340g) pappardelle pasta
- 1/2 cup (75g) sundried tomatoes, packed in oil, drained and chopped
- 2 tablespoons olive oil (from the sundried tomatoes jar)
- 2 tablespoons unsalted butter
- 4 cloves garlic, minced
- 1 cup (240ml) chicken or vegetable broth
- 1 cup (240ml) heavy cream
- 1/2 cup (50g) grated Parmesan cheese
- 1 teaspoon dried basil
- 1/2 teaspoon dried oregano
- Salt and black pepper to taste
- Fresh basil, chopped, for garnish
- Grated Parmesan cheese for serving (optional)

Instructions:

Cook the pappardelle pasta according to the package instructions in a large pot of salted boiling water. Drain and set aside.
In a large skillet, heat the olive oil (from the sundried tomatoes jar) and butter over medium heat.
Add minced garlic to the skillet and sauté for about 1-2 minutes until fragrant.
Stir in the chopped sundried tomatoes and cook for an additional 2 minutes.
Pour in the chicken or vegetable broth, heavy cream, grated Parmesan cheese, dried basil, and dried oregano. Stir well and let the mixture simmer for about 5-7 minutes, allowing it to thicken.
Season the creamy sauce with salt and black pepper to taste.
Add the cooked pappardelle pasta to the skillet, tossing to coat the pasta in the creamy sundried tomato sauce.
Garnish with chopped fresh basil and additional grated Parmesan cheese if desired.
Serve the Creamy Sundried Tomato Pappardelle immediately.

Enjoy this rich and flavorful pasta dish with a unique combination of sundried tomatoes and creamy sauce. It's a delightful and comforting meal. Buon appetito!

Spicy Sausage and Peppers Penne

Ingredients:

- 12 ounces (340g) penne pasta
- 1 pound (450g) spicy Italian sausage, casings removed
- 2 tablespoons olive oil
- 1 onion, thinly sliced
- 2 bell peppers (red and yellow), thinly sliced
- 3 cloves garlic, minced
- 1 can (14 ounces/400g) crushed tomatoes
- 1 teaspoon dried oregano
- 1 teaspoon dried basil
- 1/2 teaspoon red pepper flakes (adjust to taste)
- Salt and black pepper to taste
- 1/4 cup (60ml) heavy cream
- Fresh basil or parsley, chopped, for garnish
- Grated Parmesan cheese for serving (optional)

Instructions:

Cook the penne pasta according to the package instructions in a large pot of salted boiling water. Drain and set aside.

In a large skillet, heat olive oil over medium-high heat. Add the spicy Italian sausage, breaking it into crumbles with a spoon. Cook until browned and cooked through. Remove any excess fat.

Add thinly sliced onions and bell peppers to the skillet. Sauté until the vegetables are softened.

Stir in minced garlic and cook for an additional 1-2 minutes until fragrant.

Pour in the crushed tomatoes, dried oregano, dried basil, red pepper flakes, salt, and black pepper. Mix well and let the mixture simmer for about 10 minutes, allowing the flavors to meld.

Reduce the heat to low, pour in the heavy cream, and simmer for an additional 2-3 minutes.

Add the cooked penne pasta to the skillet, tossing to coat the pasta in the spicy sausage and peppers sauce.

Adjust the seasoning if needed.

Garnish with chopped fresh basil or parsley.

Serve the Spicy Sausage and Peppers Penne immediately.

Optionally, top with grated Parmesan cheese when serving.

Enjoy this delicious and hearty Spicy Sausage and Peppers Penne for a satisfying and flavorful meal. Pair it with a side salad or crusty bread for a complete dining experience. Buon appetito!

Shrimp and Spinach Ravioli in Tomato Cream Sauce

Ingredients:

- 1 pound (450g) shrimp, peeled and deveined
- Salt and black pepper to taste
- 2 tablespoons olive oil
- 3 cloves garlic, minced
- 1 can (14 ounces/400g) crushed tomatoes
- 1 teaspoon dried basil
- 1 teaspoon dried oregano
- 1/2 teaspoon red pepper flakes (adjust to taste)
- 1 cup (240ml) heavy cream
- 1/2 cup (50g) grated Parmesan cheese
- 1 pound (450g) fresh or frozen shrimp and spinach ravioli
- Fresh basil or parsley, chopped, for garnish
- Grated Parmesan cheese for serving (optional)

Instructions:

Season the shrimp with salt and black pepper.
In a large skillet, heat olive oil over medium-high heat. Add the shrimp and cook until they are pink and opaque. Remove from the skillet and set aside.
In the same skillet, add minced garlic and sauté for about 1-2 minutes until fragrant.
Pour in the crushed tomatoes, dried basil, dried oregano, and red pepper flakes. Stir well and let the mixture simmer for about 10 minutes.
Reduce the heat to low, pour in the heavy cream, and simmer for an additional 2-3 minutes.
Stir in the grated Parmesan cheese until the sauce is smooth and creamy.
Meanwhile, cook the shrimp and spinach ravioli according to the package instructions in a large pot of salted boiling water. Drain and set aside.
Add the cooked shrimp back to the skillet, tossing to coat them in the tomato cream sauce.
Gently fold in the cooked shrimp and spinach ravioli, ensuring they are well-coated in the creamy sauce.
Adjust the seasoning if needed.
Garnish with chopped fresh basil or parsley.
Serve the Shrimp and Spinach Ravioli in Tomato Cream Sauce immediately.

Optionally, top with additional grated Parmesan cheese when serving.

Enjoy this delightful and creamy dish featuring shrimp and spinach ravioli in a flavorful tomato cream sauce. It's a perfect combination of seafood, pasta, and rich sauce. Buon appetito!

Mushroom and Goat Cheese Farfalle

Ingredients:

- 12 ounces (340g) farfalle (bowtie) pasta
- 2 tablespoons olive oil
- 1 pound (450g) mushrooms, sliced
- 3 cloves garlic, minced
- Salt and black pepper to taste
- 1/2 cup (120ml) dry white wine (optional)
- 4 ounces (115g) goat cheese
- 1/2 cup (120ml) chicken or vegetable broth
- 1/4 cup (60ml) heavy cream
- 1/4 cup (25g) grated Parmesan cheese
- Fresh parsley, chopped, for garnish

Instructions:

Cook the farfalle pasta according to the package instructions in a large pot of salted boiling water. Drain and set aside.
In a large skillet, heat olive oil over medium heat. Add sliced mushrooms and cook until they release their moisture and become golden brown.
Add minced garlic to the skillet and sauté for an additional 1-2 minutes until fragrant.
Season the mushrooms with salt and black pepper to taste.
If using, pour in the dry white wine and let it simmer for a couple of minutes until it's reduced.
Reduce the heat to low. Crumble the goat cheese into the skillet and stir until it melts.
Pour in the chicken or vegetable broth and heavy cream. Stir well and let the mixture simmer for 3-4 minutes.
Add the cooked farfalle pasta to the skillet, tossing to coat the pasta in the creamy mushroom and goat cheese sauce.
Stir in the grated Parmesan cheese until the sauce is smooth and has a velvety texture.
Adjust the seasoning if needed.
Garnish with chopped fresh parsley.
Serve the Mushroom and Goat Cheese Farfalle immediately.

Enjoy this delightful and creamy Mushroom and Goat Cheese Farfalle as a comforting and flavorful meal. It's a perfect dish for mushroom and cheese lovers. Buon appetito!

Chicken Marsala Fettuccine

Ingredients:

- 8 ounces (225g) fettuccine pasta
- 2 boneless, skinless chicken breasts, pounded thin
- Salt and black pepper to taste
- 1/2 cup (60g) all-purpose flour, for dredging
- 4 tablespoons unsalted butter, divided
- 2 tablespoons olive oil
- 8 ounces (225g) cremini or white mushrooms, sliced
- 2 cloves garlic, minced
- 1 cup (240ml) Marsala wine
- 1 cup (240ml) chicken broth
- 1/2 cup (120ml) heavy cream
- 1 teaspoon dried thyme
- 1/4 cup (60g) grated Parmesan cheese
- Fresh parsley, chopped, for garnish

Instructions:

Cook the fettuccine pasta according to the package instructions in a large pot of salted boiling water. Drain and set aside.

Season the pounded chicken breasts with salt and black pepper. Dredge each chicken breast in flour, shaking off excess.

In a large skillet, heat 2 tablespoons of butter and olive oil over medium-high heat. Add the chicken breasts and cook until browned on both sides and cooked through. Remove the chicken from the skillet and set aside.

In the same skillet, add the remaining 2 tablespoons of butter. Add the sliced mushrooms and cook until they release their moisture and become golden brown.

Add minced garlic to the skillet and sauté for an additional 1-2 minutes until fragrant.

Pour in the Marsala wine and scrape up any browned bits from the bottom of the skillet. Let it simmer for 3-4 minutes until the wine is reduced.

Add the chicken broth, heavy cream, and dried thyme. Stir well and let the mixture simmer for 5-7 minutes until it thickens.

Slice the cooked chicken breasts into thin strips and add them back to the skillet. Stir in the grated Parmesan cheese until the sauce is smooth and creamy.

Adjust the seasoning if needed.
Add the cooked fettuccine pasta to the skillet, tossing to coat the pasta in the Chicken Marsala sauce.
Garnish with chopped fresh parsley.
Serve the Chicken Marsala Fettuccine immediately.

Enjoy this delicious and classic Chicken Marsala Fettuccine as a comforting and flavorful meal. It's perfect for a special dinner or any occasion. Buon appetito!

Creamy Garlic Parmesan Orzo

Ingredients:

- 1 cup (200g) orzo pasta
- 2 tablespoons unsalted butter
- 3 cloves garlic, minced
- 2 cups (480ml) chicken or vegetable broth
- 1 cup (240ml) heavy cream
- 1 cup (100g) grated Parmesan cheese
- Salt and black pepper to taste
- Fresh parsley, chopped, for garnish

Instructions:

Cook the orzo pasta according to the package instructions in a pot of salted boiling water. Drain and set aside.
In a large skillet, melt the butter over medium heat. Add minced garlic and sauté for about 1-2 minutes until fragrant.
Pour in the chicken or vegetable broth and heavy cream. Stir well and bring the mixture to a simmer.
Reduce the heat to low and stir in the grated Parmesan cheese. Continue stirring until the cheese is melted and the sauce is smooth.
Season the sauce with salt and black pepper to taste.
Add the cooked orzo pasta to the skillet, tossing to coat the pasta in the creamy garlic Parmesan sauce.
Adjust the seasoning if needed.
Garnish with chopped fresh parsley.
Serve the Creamy Garlic Parmesan Orzo immediately.

Enjoy this simple and delicious Creamy Garlic Parmesan Orzo as a side dish or a quick main course. The creamy sauce complements the orzo perfectly, creating a flavorful and comforting dish. Buon appetito!

Baked Spinach and Artichoke Pasta

Ingredients:

- 12 ounces (340g) penne or your favorite pasta
- 1 tablespoon olive oil
- 1 onion, finely chopped
- 3 cloves garlic, minced
- 8 ounces (225g) fresh baby spinach
- 1 can (14 ounces/400g) artichoke hearts, drained and chopped
- 1 cup (240ml) vegetable broth
- 1 cup (240ml) heavy cream
- 1 cup (100g) grated Parmesan cheese
- 1 cup (225g) ricotta cheese
- 1 teaspoon dried oregano
- 1/2 teaspoon red pepper flakes (optional, for heat)
- Salt and black pepper to taste
- 1 1/2 cups (150g) shredded mozzarella cheese
- Fresh parsley, chopped, for garnish

Instructions:

Preheat the oven to 375°F (190°C).
Cook the pasta according to the package instructions in a large pot of salted boiling water. Drain and set aside.
In a large skillet, heat olive oil over medium heat. Add chopped onion and sauté until it becomes translucent.
Add minced garlic to the skillet and cook for an additional 1-2 minutes until fragrant.
Add fresh baby spinach to the skillet and cook until wilted.
Stir in the chopped artichoke hearts, vegetable broth, heavy cream, grated Parmesan cheese, ricotta cheese, dried oregano, red pepper flakes (if using), salt, and black pepper. Mix well and let the mixture simmer for 5-7 minutes.
Add the cooked pasta to the skillet, tossing to coat the pasta in the spinach and artichoke mixture.
Transfer the pasta mixture to a greased baking dish.
Sprinkle shredded mozzarella cheese evenly over the top.

Bake in the preheated oven for 20-25 minutes, or until the cheese is melted and bubbly, and the edges are golden brown.
Remove from the oven and let it rest for a few minutes before serving.
Garnish with chopped fresh parsley.
Serve the Baked Spinach and Artichoke Pasta immediately.

Enjoy this creamy and cheesy Baked Spinach and Artichoke Pasta for a comforting and flavorful meal. It's perfect for a cozy dinner or for entertaining guests. Buon appetito!

Butternut Squash and Sage Ravioli

Ingredients:

For the Ravioli Filling:

- 2 cups (about 400g) butternut squash, peeled, seeded, and diced
- 1 tablespoon olive oil
- Salt and black pepper to taste
- 1/4 teaspoon ground nutmeg
- 1/2 cup (120g) ricotta cheese
- 1/4 cup (25g) grated Parmesan cheese

For the Sage Butter Sauce:

- 1/2 cup (115g) unsalted butter
- 1/4 cup (15g) fresh sage leaves
- Salt and black pepper to taste

For Serving:

- Freshly grated Parmesan cheese
- Toasted pine nuts (optional)
- Fresh parsley, chopped, for garnish

Instructions:

Ravioli Filling:

> Preheat the oven to 400°F (200°C).
> Toss the diced butternut squash with olive oil, salt, black pepper, and ground nutmeg.
> Spread the seasoned butternut squash on a baking sheet in a single layer.
> Roast in the preheated oven for about 25-30 minutes or until the squash is tender and caramelized. Allow it to cool slightly.
> In a food processor, combine the roasted butternut squash, ricotta cheese, and grated Parmesan cheese. Blend until smooth and well combined.

Ravioli Assembly:

Prepare the butternut squash filling and set it aside.
Lay out the fresh pasta sheets or use store-bought wonton wrappers.
Place small portions of the butternut squash filling onto the center of each pasta square.
Brush the edges of the pasta with water and fold the pasta over the filling, pressing the edges to seal and remove any air bubbles.
Use a pasta cutter or a knife to cut the ravioli into desired shapes.

Sage Butter Sauce:

In a large skillet, melt the unsalted butter over medium heat.
Add fresh sage leaves to the melted butter and sauté until the sage becomes crispy. Be careful not to burn the butter; adjust the heat as needed.
Season the sage butter with salt and black pepper to taste.

Cooking Ravioli:

Bring a large pot of salted water to a boil.
Carefully drop the ravioli into the boiling water and cook until they float to the surface, usually about 2-3 minutes for fresh ravioli.
Using a slotted spoon, remove the cooked ravioli from the water and transfer them directly to the skillet with the sage butter sauce. Gently toss to coat the ravioli in the sauce.

Serving:

Plate the Butternut Squash and Sage Ravioli, drizzling any remaining sage butter sauce over the top.
Garnish with freshly grated Parmesan cheese, toasted pine nuts (if using), and chopped fresh parsley.
Serve immediately and enjoy!

This Butternut Squash and Sage Ravioli recipe is a delicious and comforting dish, perfect for autumn or anytime you crave a flavorful pasta meal. Buon appetito!

Creamy Cajun Shrimp Linguine

Ingredients:

- 8 ounces (225g) linguine pasta
- 1 pound (450g) large shrimp, peeled and deveined
- Cajun seasoning (store-bought or homemade), to taste
- 2 tablespoons olive oil
- 4 cloves garlic, minced
- 1 red bell pepper, thinly sliced
- 1 yellow bell pepper, thinly sliced
- 1 cup (240ml) chicken broth
- 1 cup (240ml) heavy cream
- 1 teaspoon smoked paprika
- 1/2 teaspoon dried thyme
- Salt and black pepper to taste
- 1/4 cup (30g) grated Parmesan cheese
- Fresh parsley, chopped, for garnish

Instructions:

Cook the linguine pasta according to the package instructions in a large pot of salted boiling water. Drain and set aside.

Season the shrimp with Cajun seasoning, ensuring they are well-coated.

In a large skillet, heat olive oil over medium-high heat. Add the seasoned shrimp and cook until they are pink and opaque. Remove the shrimp from the skillet and set aside.

In the same skillet, add minced garlic and sauté for about 1-2 minutes until fragrant.

Add thinly sliced red and yellow bell peppers to the skillet. Cook for 2-3 minutes until the peppers are slightly softened.

Pour in the chicken broth, heavy cream, smoked paprika, dried thyme, salt, and black pepper. Stir well and let the mixture simmer for about 5-7 minutes, allowing it to thicken.

Add the cooked linguine pasta to the skillet, tossing to coat the pasta in the creamy Cajun sauce.

Gently fold in the cooked Cajun shrimp, ensuring they are well-coated in the sauce.

Stir in the grated Parmesan cheese until the sauce is smooth and has a velvety texture.
Adjust the seasoning if needed.
Garnish with chopped fresh parsley.
Serve the Creamy Cajun Shrimp Linguine immediately.

Enjoy this flavorful and creamy Cajun Shrimp Linguine for a satisfying and indulgent meal. It's a perfect combination of spices, shrimp, and creamy sauce. Buon appetito!

Caprese Stuffed Portobello Mushroom Pasta

Ingredients:

For the Stuffed Portobello Mushrooms:

- 4 large Portobello mushrooms, stems removed and cleaned
- 2 tablespoons balsamic glaze
- 1 cup (250g) fresh mozzarella, diced
- 1 cup (200g) cherry tomatoes, halved
- Fresh basil leaves, for garnish
- Salt and black pepper to taste

For the Pasta:

- 8 ounces (225g) penne or your favorite pasta
- 2 tablespoons olive oil
- 4 cloves garlic, minced
- 1 can (14 ounces/400g) crushed tomatoes
- Salt and black pepper to taste
- 1 teaspoon dried oregano
- 1/2 teaspoon red pepper flakes (optional, for heat)
- Fresh basil, chopped, for garnish

Instructions:

Stuffed Portobello Mushrooms:

    Preheat the oven to 400°F (200°C).
    Place the cleaned Portobello mushrooms on a baking sheet.
    Drizzle balsamic glaze over the mushrooms and season with salt and black pepper.
    Distribute diced mozzarella evenly among the mushrooms.
    Top each mushroom with halved cherry tomatoes.
    Bake in the preheated oven for 15-20 minutes or until the mushrooms are tender and the cheese is melted.
    Garnish the stuffed mushrooms with fresh basil leaves.

Pasta:

Cook the penne pasta according to the package instructions in a large pot of salted boiling water. Drain and set aside.

In a large skillet, heat olive oil over medium heat. Add minced garlic and sauté for about 1-2 minutes until fragrant.

Pour in the crushed tomatoes, dried oregano, and red pepper flakes (if using). Stir well and let the mixture simmer for 10-12 minutes, allowing it to thicken.

Season the sauce with salt and black pepper to taste.

Add the cooked penne pasta to the skillet, tossing to coat the pasta in the tomato sauce.

Serve the pasta on plates, placing a Caprese stuffed Portobello mushroom on top of each serving.

Garnish with additional fresh basil.

Drizzle with extra balsamic glaze if desired.

Enjoy this delightful and colorful Caprese Stuffed Portobello Mushroom Pasta for a flavorful and satisfying meal. It's a perfect blend of pasta, tomatoes, mozzarella, and balsamic goodness. Buon appetito!

Chicken and Broccoli Alfredo

Ingredients:

- 8 ounces (225g) fettuccine pasta
- 2 tablespoons unsalted butter
- 1 pound (450g) boneless, skinless chicken breasts, cut into bite-sized pieces
- Salt and black pepper to taste
- 3 cloves garlic, minced
- 2 cups (200g) broccoli florets
- 1 cup (240ml) chicken broth
- 1 cup (240ml) heavy cream
- 1 cup (100g) grated Parmesan cheese
- 1/2 teaspoon dried oregano
- 1/4 teaspoon nutmeg
- Fresh parsley, chopped, for garnish

Instructions:

Cook the fettuccine pasta according to the package instructions in a large pot of salted boiling water. Drain and set aside.

In a large skillet, melt the butter over medium-high heat. Add the chicken pieces and season with salt and black pepper. Cook until the chicken is browned and cooked through. Remove the chicken from the skillet and set aside.

In the same skillet, add minced garlic and sauté for about 1-2 minutes until fragrant.

Add broccoli florets to the skillet and cook for an additional 2-3 minutes until they are slightly tender.

Pour in the chicken broth and heavy cream. Stir well and let the mixture simmer for about 5-7 minutes, allowing it to thicken.

Stir in the grated Parmesan cheese until the sauce is smooth and creamy.

Add the cooked fettuccine pasta and chicken back to the skillet, tossing to coat the pasta and chicken in the Alfredo sauce.

Season the dish with dried oregano and nutmeg. Adjust the seasoning if needed.

Garnish with chopped fresh parsley.

Serve the Chicken and Broccoli Alfredo immediately.

Enjoy this creamy and satisfying Chicken and Broccoli Alfredo for a comforting and flavorful meal. It's a classic combination of tender chicken, broccoli, and rich Alfredo sauce. Buon appetito!

Brown Butter and Sage Gnocchi

Ingredients:

- 1 pound (450g) store-bought or homemade gnocchi
- 1/2 cup (115g) unsalted butter
- Fresh sage leaves (about 10-12 leaves)
- Salt and black pepper to taste
- Grated Parmesan cheese, for serving
- Optional: Chopped fresh parsley for garnish

Instructions:

Cook the gnocchi according to the package instructions or prepare homemade gnocchi.
In a large skillet, melt the unsalted butter over medium heat. Once melted, continue to cook the butter until it turns golden brown, and you start to smell a nutty aroma. Be attentive and swirl the butter in the pan to prevent burning.
Add fresh sage leaves to the browned butter and fry for about 1-2 minutes until the sage becomes crispy. Remove some sage leaves for garnish if desired.
Carefully add the cooked gnocchi to the skillet, tossing gently to coat the gnocchi in the brown butter and sage sauce. Allow the gnocchi to cook for an additional 2-3 minutes, allowing them to become slightly crispy on the edges.
Season the gnocchi with salt and black pepper to taste.
Serve the Brown Butter and Sage Gnocchi on plates, garnishing with additional crispy sage leaves and grated Parmesan cheese.
Optionally, sprinkle with chopped fresh parsley for added color and freshness.
Enjoy your delicious Brown Butter and Sage Gnocchi immediately!

This simple and flavorful dish highlights the nutty richness of browned butter and the aromatic essence of sage. It's a quick and delightful way to enjoy gnocchi. Buon appetito!

Tomato and Basil Pesto Spaghetti

Ingredients:

- 8 ounces (225g) spaghetti
- 2 tablespoons olive oil
- 4 cloves garlic, minced
- 1 can (14 ounces/400g) diced tomatoes, drained
- Salt and black pepper to taste
- 1/2 cup (120ml) tomato sauce
- 1/4 cup (60g) basil pesto (store-bought or homemade)
- Red pepper flakes (optional, for heat)
- Grated Parmesan cheese, for serving
- Fresh basil leaves, chopped, for garnish

Instructions:

Cook the spaghetti according to the package instructions in a large pot of salted boiling water. Drain and set aside.

In a large skillet, heat olive oil over medium heat. Add minced garlic and sauté for about 1-2 minutes until fragrant.

Add the drained diced tomatoes to the skillet, and cook for an additional 2-3 minutes until they are slightly softened.

Season the tomatoes with salt and black pepper to taste.

Stir in the tomato sauce and let the mixture simmer for 5-7 minutes, allowing the flavors to meld.

Add the cooked spaghetti to the skillet, tossing to coat the pasta in the tomato sauce.

In a small bowl, mix the basil pesto with a bit of olive oil to make it more pourable.

Drizzle the basil pesto over the spaghetti and toss until the pasta is evenly coated.

If desired, add red pepper flakes for a bit of heat.

Serve the Tomato and Basil Pesto Spaghetti on plates, garnishing with grated Parmesan cheese and chopped fresh basil.

Enjoy your delicious Tomato and Basil Pesto Spaghetti!

This flavorful pasta dish combines the freshness of tomatoes with the aromatic essence of basil pesto, creating a delightful and quick meal. Buon appetito!

Smoky Bacon Carbonara

Ingredients:

- 8 ounces (225g) spaghetti
- 1 tablespoon olive oil
- 8 slices of bacon, chopped
- 4 cloves garlic, minced
- 3 large eggs
- 1 cup (100g) grated Pecorino Romano cheese
- 1/2 cup (50g) grated Parmesan cheese
- Salt and black pepper to taste
- Fresh parsley, chopped, for garnish

Instructions:

Cook the spaghetti according to the package instructions in a large pot of salted boiling water. Drain and set aside.

In a large skillet, heat olive oil over medium heat. Add the chopped bacon and cook until it becomes crispy.

Add minced garlic to the skillet and sauté for about 1-2 minutes until fragrant.

In a bowl, whisk together the eggs, grated Pecorino Romano cheese, and grated Parmesan cheese until well combined.

Quickly toss the cooked spaghetti in the skillet with the bacon and garlic, ensuring the spaghetti is well coated in the bacon fat.

Remove the skillet from the heat, and quickly pour the egg and cheese mixture over the spaghetti, tossing continuously to create a creamy carbonara sauce. The heat from the spaghetti will cook the eggs and create a creamy texture.

Season the carbonara with salt and black pepper to taste.

Garnish with chopped fresh parsley.

Serve the Smoky Bacon Carbonara immediately.

Enjoy this classic and indulgent Smoky Bacon Carbonara with its rich and creamy sauce complemented by the savory goodness of bacon. Buon appetito!

Chicken and Mushroom Farfalle

Ingredients:

- 8 ounces (225g) farfalle (bowtie) pasta
- 2 tablespoons olive oil
- 1 pound (450g) boneless, skinless chicken breasts, cut into bite-sized pieces
- Salt and black pepper to taste
- 8 ounces (225g) mushrooms, sliced
- 3 cloves garlic, minced
- 1 cup (240ml) chicken broth
- 1 cup (240ml) heavy cream
- 1 teaspoon dried thyme
- 1/2 cup (50g) grated Parmesan cheese
- Fresh parsley, chopped, for garnish

Instructions:

Cook the farfalle pasta according to the package instructions in a large pot of salted boiling water. Drain and set aside.
In a large skillet, heat olive oil over medium-high heat. Add the chicken pieces and season with salt and black pepper. Cook until the chicken is browned and cooked through. Remove the chicken from the skillet and set aside.
In the same skillet, add sliced mushrooms and cook until they release their moisture and become golden brown.
Add minced garlic to the skillet and sauté for an additional 1-2 minutes until fragrant.
Pour in the chicken broth, heavy cream, and dried thyme. Stir well and let the mixture simmer for about 5-7 minutes, allowing it to thicken.
Stir in the grated Parmesan cheese until the sauce is smooth and creamy.
Add the cooked farfalle pasta to the skillet, tossing to coat the pasta in the chicken and mushroom sauce.
Gently fold in the cooked chicken, ensuring it is well-coated in the creamy sauce.
Adjust the seasoning if needed.
Garnish with chopped fresh parsley.
Serve the Chicken and Mushroom Farfalle immediately.

Enjoy this delicious and creamy Chicken and Mushroom Farfalle for a comforting and satisfying meal. It's a perfect combination of tender chicken, savory mushrooms, and a rich cream sauce. Buon appetito!

Creamy Lemon and Asparagus Tagliatelle

Ingredients:

- 8 ounces (225g) tagliatelle pasta
- 2 tablespoons unsalted butter
- 1 bunch fresh asparagus, tough ends trimmed and cut into bite-sized pieces
- 3 cloves garlic, minced
- Zest of 1 lemon
- 1 cup (240ml) chicken or vegetable broth
- 1 cup (240ml) heavy cream
- Juice of 1 lemon
- Salt and black pepper to taste
- 1/2 cup (50g) grated Parmesan cheese
- Fresh parsley, chopped, for garnish

Instructions:

Cook the tagliatelle pasta according to the package instructions in a large pot of salted boiling water. Drain and set aside.
In a large skillet, melt the butter over medium heat. Add the asparagus pieces and sauté until they are slightly tender.
Add minced garlic to the skillet and sauté for about 1-2 minutes until fragrant.
Sprinkle lemon zest over the asparagus and garlic, stirring to combine.
Pour in the chicken or vegetable broth and heavy cream. Stir well and let the mixture simmer for about 5-7 minutes, allowing it to thicken.
Add the cooked tagliatelle pasta to the skillet, tossing to coat the pasta in the creamy asparagus sauce.
Squeeze the juice of one lemon into the skillet, stirring to incorporate the lemon flavor.
Season the dish with salt and black pepper to taste.
Stir in the grated Parmesan cheese until the sauce is smooth and has a velvety texture.
Adjust the seasoning if needed.
Garnish with chopped fresh parsley.
Serve the Creamy Lemon and Asparagus Tagliatelle immediately.

Enjoy this delightful and refreshing Creamy Lemon and Asparagus Tagliatelle for a light and flavorful meal. It's a perfect combination of creamy sauce, bright lemon, and tender asparagus. Buon appetito!

Pumpkin Sage Alfredo with Orecchiette

Ingredients:

- 8 ounces (225g) orecchiette pasta
- 2 tablespoons unsalted butter
- 2 cloves garlic, minced
- 1 cup (240ml) canned pumpkin puree
- 1 cup (240ml) heavy cream
- 1/2 cup (50g) grated Parmesan cheese
- 1/2 teaspoon dried sage
- Salt and black pepper to taste
- Pinch of nutmeg
- Fresh sage leaves, for garnish

Instructions:

Cook the orecchiette pasta according to the package instructions in a large pot of salted boiling water. Drain and set aside.
In a large skillet, melt the butter over medium heat. Add minced garlic and sauté for about 1-2 minutes until fragrant.
Stir in the canned pumpkin puree, heavy cream, grated Parmesan cheese, dried sage, salt, black pepper, and nutmeg. Mix well.
Let the sauce simmer for 5-7 minutes, allowing it to thicken and the flavors to meld.
Add the cooked orecchiette pasta to the skillet, tossing to coat the pasta in the creamy pumpkin sage Alfredo sauce.
Adjust the seasoning if needed.
Garnish with fresh sage leaves.
Serve the Pumpkin Sage Alfredo with Orecchiette immediately.

Enjoy this comforting and seasonal Pumpkin Sage Alfredo with Orecchiette. The creamy pumpkin sauce with hints of sage and nutmeg adds a delightful autumn touch to your pasta dish. Buon appetito!

Seafood Fra Diavolo Linguine

Ingredients:

- 8 ounces (225g) linguine pasta
- 2 tablespoons olive oil
- 4 cloves garlic, minced
- 1 teaspoon red pepper flakes (adjust to taste for spice level)
- 1 can (14 ounces/400g) crushed tomatoes
- 1/2 cup (120ml) dry white wine
- 1/2 cup (120ml) seafood or fish stock
- 1 pound (450g) mixed seafood (shrimp, scallops, mussels, etc.)
- Salt and black pepper to taste
- 2 tablespoons fresh parsley, chopped
- 1 tablespoon fresh basil, chopped
- Lemon wedges, for serving

Instructions:

Cook the linguine pasta according to the package instructions in a large pot of salted boiling water. Drain and set aside.

In a large skillet, heat olive oil over medium heat. Add minced garlic and red pepper flakes. Sauté for about 1-2 minutes until fragrant.

Pour in the crushed tomatoes, dry white wine, and seafood or fish stock. Stir well and bring the mixture to a simmer.

Add the mixed seafood to the skillet, ensuring they are submerged in the sauce. Cover the skillet and let it simmer for 5-7 minutes or until the seafood is cooked through.

Season the sauce with salt and black pepper to taste.

Add the cooked linguine pasta to the skillet, tossing to coat the pasta in the Seafood Fra Diavolo sauce.

Stir in chopped fresh parsley and basil. Mix well.

Adjust the seasoning if needed.

Serve the Seafood Fra Diavolo Linguine immediately, garnished with additional fresh herbs.

Provide lemon wedges on the side for squeezing over the seafood.

Enjoy this spicy and flavorful Seafood Fra Diavolo Linguine for a delightful seafood pasta experience. Buon appetito!

Spinach and Feta Stuffed Shells

Ingredients:

For the Stuffed Shells:

- 24 jumbo pasta shells
- 2 tablespoons olive oil
- 1 small onion, finely chopped
- 3 cloves garlic, minced
- 1 (10-ounce/280g) package frozen chopped spinach, thawed and squeezed dry
- 1 cup (250g) ricotta cheese
- 1 cup (100g) crumbled feta cheese
- 1/2 cup (50g) grated Parmesan cheese
- 1 egg
- Salt and black pepper to taste

For the Tomato Sauce:

- 1 can (28 ounces/800g) crushed tomatoes
- 2 tablespoons tomato paste
- 2 cloves garlic, minced
- 1 teaspoon dried oregano
- 1 teaspoon dried basil
- Salt and black pepper to taste

For Baking:

- 1 1/2 cups (150g) shredded mozzarella cheese
- Fresh parsley, chopped, for garnish

Instructions:

Prepare the Tomato Sauce:

In a saucepan, combine crushed tomatoes, tomato paste, minced garlic, dried oregano, dried basil, salt, and black pepper.

Simmer the sauce over medium heat for 15-20 minutes, stirring occasionally. Adjust seasoning if needed.

Prepare the Stuffed Shells:

Cook the jumbo pasta shells according to the package instructions in a large pot of salted boiling water. Drain and set aside.
In a skillet, heat olive oil over medium heat. Add chopped onion and sauté until softened.
Add minced garlic to the skillet and cook for an additional 1-2 minutes until fragrant.
In a large bowl, combine the thawed and squeezed dry chopped spinach, ricotta cheese, feta cheese, Parmesan cheese, sautéed onion, garlic, egg, salt, and black pepper. Mix well.
Preheat the oven to 375°F (190°C).
Stuff each cooked pasta shell with the spinach and feta mixture.
Spread a thin layer of the prepared tomato sauce in the bottom of a baking dish.
Arrange the stuffed shells in the baking dish.
Pour the remaining tomato sauce over the stuffed shells.
Sprinkle shredded mozzarella cheese over the top.
Cover the baking dish with foil and bake in the preheated oven for 25 minutes.
Remove the foil and bake for an additional 10-15 minutes until the cheese is melted and bubbly, and the edges are golden brown.
Garnish with chopped fresh parsley.
Serve the Spinach and Feta Stuffed Shells hot.

Enjoy this delicious and cheesy Spinach and Feta Stuffed Shells for a comforting and satisfying meal. Buon appetito!

Creamy Chipotle Chicken Penne

Ingredients:

- 8 ounces (225g) penne pasta
- 2 tablespoons olive oil
- 1 pound (450g) boneless, skinless chicken breasts, cut into bite-sized pieces
- Salt and black pepper to taste
- 1 small onion, finely chopped
- 3 cloves garlic, minced
- 1 can (14 ounces/400g) diced tomatoes, drained
- 1-2 chipotle peppers in adobo sauce, minced (adjust to taste for spice level)
- 1 cup (240ml) chicken broth
- 1 cup (240ml) heavy cream
- 1 teaspoon ground cumin
- 1 teaspoon smoked paprika
- 1 cup (100g) shredded Monterey Jack or Mexican blend cheese
- Fresh cilantro, chopped, for garnish
- Lime wedges, for serving

Instructions:

Cook the penne pasta according to the package instructions in a large pot of salted boiling water. Drain and set aside.

In a large skillet, heat olive oil over medium-high heat. Season the chicken pieces with salt and black pepper, then cook until browned and cooked through. Remove the chicken from the skillet and set aside.

In the same skillet, add chopped onion and sauté until it becomes translucent. Add minced garlic to the skillet and cook for an additional 1-2 minutes until fragrant.

Stir in the diced tomatoes and chipotle peppers in adobo sauce. Cook for 2-3 minutes.

Pour in the chicken broth, heavy cream, ground cumin, and smoked paprika. Stir well and let the mixture simmer for about 5-7 minutes, allowing it to thicken.

Add the cooked penne pasta and browned chicken to the skillet, tossing to coat the pasta and chicken in the creamy chipotle sauce.

Stir in the shredded Monterey Jack or Mexican blend cheese until melted and the sauce is smooth.

Adjust the seasoning if needed.
Garnish with chopped fresh cilantro.
Serve the Creamy Chipotle Chicken Penne hot, with lime wedges on the side for squeezing over the dish.

Enjoy this flavorful and slightly spicy Creamy Chipotle Chicken Penne for a delicious and satisfying meal. Buon appetito!

Roasted Vegetable and Goat Cheese Lasagna

Ingredients:

For the Roasted Vegetables:

- 2 zucchini, sliced
- 1 eggplant, sliced
- 1 bell pepper, thinly sliced
- 1 red onion, thinly sliced
- 3 tablespoons olive oil
- Salt and black pepper to taste
- 1 teaspoon dried Italian herbs (oregano, thyme, basil)

For the Goat Cheese Filling:

- 8 ounces (225g) goat cheese, softened
- 1 cup (240ml) ricotta cheese
- 1/2 cup (50g) grated Parmesan cheese
- 1 egg
- Salt and black pepper to taste

Other Ingredients:

- 9 lasagna noodles, cooked according to package instructions
- 3 cups (720ml) marinara sauce
- 2 cups (200g) shredded mozzarella cheese
- Fresh basil, chopped, for garnish

Instructions:

Roasted Vegetables:

Preheat the oven to 400°F (200°C).
In a large bowl, toss the sliced zucchini, eggplant, bell pepper, and red onion with olive oil, salt, black pepper, and dried Italian herbs.
Spread the vegetables on a baking sheet in a single layer.

Roast in the preheated oven for about 20-25 minutes or until the vegetables are tender and slightly caramelized. Set aside.

Goat Cheese Filling:

In a bowl, combine the softened goat cheese, ricotta cheese, grated Parmesan cheese, egg, salt, and black pepper. Mix until well combined.

Assembly:

Preheat the oven to 375°F (190°C).
In a baking dish, spread a thin layer of marinara sauce.
Place three cooked lasagna noodles over the sauce.
Spread half of the goat cheese filling over the noodles.
Layer half of the roasted vegetables over the goat cheese filling.
Sprinkle a portion of shredded mozzarella cheese over the vegetables.
Repeat the layers with three more lasagna noodles, the remaining goat cheese filling, the remaining roasted vegetables, and another portion of shredded mozzarella cheese.
Top with the final three lasagna noodles and cover with the remaining marinara sauce.
Sprinkle the remaining shredded mozzarella cheese over the top.
Cover the baking dish with foil and bake in the preheated oven for 30 minutes.
Remove the foil and bake for an additional 15-20 minutes or until the cheese is melted and bubbly, and the edges are golden brown.
Let the lasagna rest for 10 minutes before slicing.
Garnish with chopped fresh basil.
Serve the Roasted Vegetable and Goat Cheese Lasagna warm.

Enjoy this flavorful and veggie-packed Roasted Vegetable and Goat Cheese Lasagna for a satisfying and comforting meal. Buon appetito!

Lemon Garlic Butter Shrimp Linguine

Ingredients:

- 8 ounces (225g) linguine pasta
- 1 pound (450g) large shrimp, peeled and deveined
- Salt and black pepper to taste
- 3 tablespoons unsalted butter
- 4 cloves garlic, minced
- Zest of 1 lemon
- Juice of 1 lemon
- 1/2 cup (120ml) chicken broth
- 1/4 cup (60ml) heavy cream
- 1/4 cup (30g) grated Parmesan cheese
- Fresh parsley, chopped, for garnish

Instructions:

Cook the linguine pasta according to the package instructions in a large pot of salted boiling water. Drain and set aside.
Season the shrimp with salt and black pepper to taste.
In a large skillet, melt 2 tablespoons of butter over medium-high heat. Add the shrimp and cook until they are pink and opaque. Remove the shrimp from the skillet and set aside.
In the same skillet, add the remaining 1 tablespoon of butter. Add minced garlic and sauté for about 1-2 minutes until fragrant.
Pour in the chicken broth, heavy cream, lemon zest, and lemon juice. Stir well and let the mixture simmer for about 3-5 minutes, allowing it to thicken.
Stir in the grated Parmesan cheese until the sauce is smooth and creamy.
Add the cooked linguine pasta to the skillet, tossing to coat the pasta in the lemon garlic butter sauce.
Gently fold in the cooked shrimp, ensuring they are well-coated in the sauce.
Adjust the seasoning if needed.
Garnish with chopped fresh parsley.
Serve the Lemon Garlic Butter Shrimp Linguine immediately.

Enjoy this delightful and zesty Lemon Garlic Butter Shrimp Linguine for a light and flavorful meal. The combination of shrimp, garlic, and lemon creates a refreshing and satisfying dish. Buon appetito!

Sundried Tomato and Basil Pesto Cavatelli

Ingredients:

- 8 ounces (225g) cavatelli pasta
- 1/2 cup (120ml) sundried tomatoes in oil, drained and chopped
- 1/2 cup (60g) pine nuts
- 2 cups (50g) fresh basil leaves
- 3 cloves garlic, minced
- 1/2 cup (50g) grated Parmesan cheese
- 1/2 cup (120ml) extra-virgin olive oil
- Salt and black pepper to taste
- Crushed red pepper flakes (optional, for heat)
- Grated Pecorino Romano cheese, for serving
- Fresh basil leaves, for garnish

Instructions:

Cook the cavatelli pasta according to the package instructions in a large pot of salted boiling water. Drain and set aside.
In a food processor, combine the sundried tomatoes, pine nuts, fresh basil, minced garlic, and grated Parmesan cheese.
Pulse the ingredients until finely chopped.
With the food processor running, slowly pour in the extra-virgin olive oil until the mixture forms a smooth pesto sauce.
Season the pesto with salt and black pepper to taste. Add crushed red pepper flakes if you desire a bit of heat.
In a large mixing bowl, toss the cooked cavatelli pasta with the Sundried Tomato and Basil Pesto until the pasta is evenly coated.
Adjust the seasoning if needed.
Serve the Sundried Tomato and Basil Pesto Cavatelli on plates, garnishing with grated Pecorino Romano cheese and fresh basil leaves.

Enjoy this flavorful and vibrant Sundried Tomato and Basil Pesto Cavatelli for a delicious and aromatic pasta dish. Buon appetito!

Beef and Spinach Stuffed Shells

Ingredients:

For the Stuffed Shells:

- 20 jumbo pasta shells
- 1 tablespoon olive oil
- 1 pound (450g) ground beef
- 1 small onion, finely chopped
- 3 cloves garlic, minced
- 1 cup (100g) fresh spinach, chopped
- 1 cup (250g) ricotta cheese
- 1 cup (100g) shredded mozzarella cheese
- 1/2 cup (50g) grated Parmesan cheese
- 1 egg
- Salt and black pepper to taste

For the Tomato Sauce:

- 2 cans (14 ounces/400g each) crushed tomatoes
- 2 cloves garlic, minced
- 1 teaspoon dried oregano
- 1 teaspoon dried basil
- Salt and black pepper to taste

For Baking:

- 1 1/2 cups (150g) shredded mozzarella cheese
- Fresh parsley, chopped, for garnish

Instructions:

Prepare the Tomato Sauce:

> In a saucepan, combine crushed tomatoes, minced garlic, dried oregano, dried basil, salt, and black pepper.

Simmer the sauce over medium heat for 15-20 minutes, stirring occasionally. Adjust seasoning if needed.

Prepare the Stuffed Shells:

Cook the jumbo pasta shells according to the package instructions in a large pot of salted boiling water. Drain and set aside.
In a skillet, heat olive oil over medium-high heat. Add chopped onion and sauté until it becomes translucent.
Add minced garlic to the skillet and cook for an additional 1-2 minutes until fragrant.
Add ground beef to the skillet and cook until browned. Drain any excess fat.
In a large bowl, combine the cooked beef, chopped spinach, ricotta cheese, shredded mozzarella cheese, grated Parmesan cheese, egg, salt, and black pepper. Mix until well combined.

Assembly:

Preheat the oven to 375°F (190°C).
Spread a thin layer of the prepared tomato sauce in the bottom of a baking dish.
Stuff each cooked pasta shell with the beef and spinach mixture.
Arrange the stuffed shells in the baking dish.
Pour the remaining tomato sauce over the stuffed shells.
Sprinkle shredded mozzarella cheese over the top.
Cover the baking dish with foil and bake in the preheated oven for 25 minutes.
Remove the foil and bake for an additional 10-15 minutes until the cheese is melted and bubbly, and the edges are golden brown.
Garnish with chopped fresh parsley.
Serve the Beef and Spinach Stuffed Shells warm.

Enjoy this hearty and cheesy Beef and Spinach Stuffed Shells for a comforting and satisfying meal. Buon appetito!

Mushroom and Thyme Tagliatelle

Ingredients:

- 8 ounces (225g) tagliatelle pasta
- 2 tablespoons olive oil
- 1 pound (450g) mixed mushrooms (such as cremini, shiitake, and oyster), sliced
- 3 cloves garlic, minced
- 1 teaspoon fresh thyme leaves
- Salt and black pepper to taste
- 1/2 cup (120ml) dry white wine
- 1 cup (240ml) chicken or vegetable broth
- 1/2 cup (120ml) heavy cream
- 1/2 cup (50g) grated Parmesan cheese
- Fresh parsley, chopped, for garnish

Instructions:

Cook the tagliatelle pasta according to the package instructions in a large pot of salted boiling water. Drain and set aside.
In a large skillet, heat olive oil over medium-high heat. Add sliced mushrooms and cook until they release their moisture and become golden brown.
Add minced garlic and fresh thyme leaves to the skillet. Sauté for about 1-2 minutes until fragrant.
Season the mushrooms with salt and black pepper to taste.
Pour in the dry white wine, stirring to deglaze the pan and cook for an additional 2-3 minutes until the wine has reduced.
Add the chicken or vegetable broth to the skillet and let the mixture simmer for about 5 minutes.
Stir in the heavy cream and grated Parmesan cheese until the sauce is smooth and creamy.
Add the cooked tagliatelle pasta to the skillet, tossing to coat the pasta in the mushroom and thyme sauce.
Adjust the seasoning if needed.
Garnish with chopped fresh parsley.
Serve the Mushroom and Thyme Tagliatelle immediately.

Enjoy this flavorful and earthy Mushroom and Thyme Tagliatelle for a comforting and aromatic pasta dish. Buon appetito!

Mediterranean Chickpea Pasta Salad

Ingredients:

For the Salad:

- 8 ounces (225g) rotini or penne pasta
- 1 can (15 ounces/425g) chickpeas, drained and rinsed
- 1 cup cherry tomatoes, halved
- 1 cucumber, diced
- 1/2 red onion, finely chopped
- 1/2 cup Kalamata olives, sliced
- 1/2 cup feta cheese, crumbled
- 1/4 cup fresh parsley, chopped

For the Dressing:

- 1/4 cup extra-virgin olive oil
- 2 tablespoons red wine vinegar
- 1 clove garlic, minced
- 1 teaspoon dried oregano
- Salt and black pepper to taste
- Lemon zest (optional, for extra freshness)

Instructions:

Cook the pasta according to the package instructions in a large pot of salted boiling water. Drain and set aside.
In a large mixing bowl, combine the cooked pasta, chickpeas, cherry tomatoes, cucumber, red onion, Kalamata olives, feta cheese, and fresh parsley.
In a small bowl, whisk together the extra-virgin olive oil, red wine vinegar, minced garlic, dried oregano, salt, and black pepper. Add lemon zest if desired.
Pour the dressing over the pasta salad and toss gently to coat all the ingredients evenly.
Refrigerate the Mediterranean Chickpea Pasta Salad for at least 30 minutes to allow the flavors to meld.
Before serving, give the salad a final toss and adjust the seasoning if needed.

Garnish with additional fresh parsley.
Serve the Mediterranean Chickpea Pasta Salad chilled.

Enjoy this refreshing and vibrant Mediterranean Chickpea Pasta Salad, perfect for a light and healthy meal. Buon appetito!

Creamy Bacon and Pea Farfalle

Ingredients:

- 8 ounces (225g) farfalle (bowtie) pasta
- 6 slices bacon, chopped
- 1 cup frozen peas
- 2 tablespoons unsalted butter
- 3 cloves garlic, minced
- 1 cup (240ml) heavy cream
- 1/2 cup (50g) grated Parmesan cheese
- Salt and black pepper to taste
- Fresh parsley, chopped, for garnish

Instructions:

Cook the farfalle pasta according to the package instructions in a large pot of salted boiling water. Drain and set aside.
In a large skillet, cook the chopped bacon over medium heat until it becomes crispy. Remove the bacon from the skillet and set aside on a paper towel to drain.
In the same skillet, add frozen peas and sauté for a few minutes until they are heated through. Remove the peas from the skillet and set aside.
In the skillet, melt butter over medium heat. Add minced garlic and sauté for about 1-2 minutes until fragrant.
Pour in the heavy cream and bring it to a simmer. Reduce heat to low.
Stir in the grated Parmesan cheese until the sauce is smooth and creamy.
Add the cooked farfalle pasta, crispy bacon, and sautéed peas to the skillet, tossing to coat the pasta in the creamy bacon and pea sauce.
Season with salt and black pepper to taste.
Adjust the seasoning if needed.
Garnish with chopped fresh parsley.
Serve the Creamy Bacon and Pea Farfalle immediately.

Enjoy this indulgent and flavorful Creamy Bacon and Pea Farfalle for a comforting and satisfying pasta dish. Buon appetito!

Chicken and Broccolini Orecchiette

Ingredients:

- 8 ounces (225g) orecchiette pasta
- 1 pound (450g) boneless, skinless chicken breasts, cut into bite-sized pieces
- Salt and black pepper to taste
- 2 tablespoons olive oil
- 3 cloves garlic, minced
- 1 bunch broccolini, trimmed and cut into bite-sized pieces
- 1 cup (240ml) chicken broth
- Zest and juice of 1 lemon
- 1/2 cup (120ml) heavy cream
- 1/2 cup (50g) grated Parmesan cheese
- Red pepper flakes (optional, for heat)
- Fresh parsley, chopped, for garnish

Instructions:

Cook the orecchiette pasta according to the package instructions in a large pot of salted boiling water. Drain and set aside.
Season the chicken pieces with salt and black pepper to taste.
In a large skillet, heat olive oil over medium-high heat. Add the seasoned chicken and cook until browned and cooked through. Remove the chicken from the skillet and set aside.
In the same skillet, add minced garlic and sauté for about 1-2 minutes until fragrant.
Add broccolini to the skillet and sauté until it is bright green and slightly tender.
Pour in the chicken broth and bring it to a simmer. Allow the broccolini to cook for an additional 3-5 minutes until it's tender-crisp.
Add the cooked chicken back to the skillet.
Stir in the lemon zest and juice, heavy cream, and grated Parmesan cheese. Add red pepper flakes if you desire a bit of heat.
Let the mixture simmer for about 5 minutes, allowing the sauce to thicken.
Add the cooked orecchiette pasta to the skillet, tossing to coat the pasta in the chicken and broccolini sauce.
Adjust the seasoning if needed.
Garnish with chopped fresh parsley.

Serve the Chicken and Broccolini Orecchiette immediately.

Enjoy this delicious and vibrant Chicken and Broccolini Orecchiette for a wholesome and flavorful meal. Buon appetito!

Sun-Dried Tomato and Artichoke Pesto Rigatoni

Ingredients:

- 8 ounces (225g) rigatoni pasta
- 1 cup sun-dried tomatoes (packed in oil), drained
- 1 cup marinated artichoke hearts, drained
- 1/2 cup fresh basil leaves
- 1/3 cup pine nuts
- 2 cloves garlic, minced
- 1/2 cup (50g) grated Parmesan cheese
- 1/2 cup (120ml) extra-virgin olive oil
- Salt and black pepper to taste
- Crushed red pepper flakes (optional, for heat)
- Grated Pecorino Romano cheese, for serving
- Fresh basil leaves, for garnish

Instructions:

Cook the rigatoni pasta according to the package instructions in a large pot of salted boiling water. Drain and set aside.

In a food processor, combine the sun-dried tomatoes, marinated artichoke hearts, fresh basil leaves, pine nuts, minced garlic, and grated Parmesan cheese. Pulse the ingredients until finely chopped.

With the food processor running, slowly pour in the extra-virgin olive oil until the mixture forms a smooth pesto.

Season the pesto with salt and black pepper to taste. Add crushed red pepper flakes if you desire a bit of heat.

In a large mixing bowl, toss the cooked rigatoni pasta with the Sun-Dried Tomato and Artichoke Pesto until the pasta is evenly coated.

Adjust the seasoning if needed.

Serve the Sun-Dried Tomato and Artichoke Pesto Rigatoni on plates, garnishing with grated Pecorino Romano cheese and fresh basil leaves.

Enjoy this flavorful and Mediterranean-inspired Sun-Dried Tomato and Artichoke Pesto Rigatoni. Buon appetito!

Spicy Sausage and Kale Penne

Ingredients:

- 8 ounces (225g) penne pasta
- 1 tablespoon olive oil
- 1 pound (450g) spicy Italian sausage, casings removed
- 1 small onion, finely chopped
- 3 cloves garlic, minced
- 1 bunch kale, stems removed and leaves chopped
- 1 can (14 ounces/400g) diced tomatoes, undrained
- 1/2 cup (120ml) chicken broth
- 1 teaspoon dried red pepper flakes (adjust to taste for spice level)
- Salt and black pepper to taste
- Grated Parmesan cheese, for serving

Instructions:

Cook the penne pasta according to the package instructions in a large pot of salted boiling water. Drain and set aside.
In a large skillet, heat olive oil over medium-high heat. Add the spicy Italian sausage, breaking it up with a spoon, and cook until browned and cooked through.
Add chopped onion to the skillet and sauté until it becomes translucent.
Add minced garlic to the skillet and cook for an additional 1-2 minutes until fragrant.
Stir in the chopped kale and cook until it wilts.
Pour in the diced tomatoes with their juice and chicken broth. Add dried red pepper flakes, salt, and black pepper to taste. Stir well.
Let the mixture simmer for about 10-15 minutes, allowing the flavors to meld and the kale to cook down.
Add the cooked penne pasta to the skillet, tossing to coat the pasta in the spicy sausage and kale sauce.
Adjust the seasoning if needed.
Serve the Spicy Sausage and Kale Penne hot, garnished with grated Parmesan cheese.

Enjoy this hearty and flavorful Spicy Sausage and Kale Penne for a delicious and satisfying pasta dish. Buon appetito!

Lemon Ricotta Stuffed Shells with Spinach

Ingredients:

For the Stuffed Shells:

- 20 jumbo pasta shells
- 1 cup ricotta cheese
- 1 cup shredded mozzarella cheese
- 1/2 cup grated Parmesan cheese
- 1 egg
- Zest of 1 lemon
- 1 cup fresh spinach, chopped
- Salt and black pepper to taste

For the Lemon Cream Sauce:

- 1/4 cup unsalted butter
- 2 cloves garlic, minced
- 1 cup heavy cream
- 1/2 cup chicken broth
- Juice of 1 lemon
- Salt and black pepper to taste

For Baking:

- 1 cup shredded mozzarella cheese
- Fresh parsley, chopped, for garnish

Instructions:

Prepare the Stuffed Shells:

Cook the jumbo pasta shells according to the package instructions in a large pot of salted boiling water. Drain and set aside.

In a large bowl, combine ricotta cheese, shredded mozzarella cheese, grated Parmesan cheese, egg, lemon zest, chopped fresh spinach, salt, and black pepper. Mix until well combined.
Preheat the oven to 375°F (190°C).
Stuff each cooked pasta shell with the lemon ricotta and spinach mixture.

Prepare the Lemon Cream Sauce:

In a saucepan, melt unsalted butter over medium heat. Add minced garlic and sauté for about 1-2 minutes until fragrant.
Pour in the heavy cream and chicken broth. Stir well.
Add the lemon juice, salt, and black pepper to the sauce. Continue to simmer for about 5-7 minutes until the sauce thickens slightly.

Assembly and Baking:

Spread a thin layer of the lemon cream sauce in the bottom of a baking dish.
Arrange the stuffed shells in the baking dish.
Pour the remaining lemon cream sauce over the stuffed shells.
Sprinkle shredded mozzarella cheese over the top.
Cover the baking dish with foil and bake in the preheated oven for 25 minutes.
Remove the foil and bake for an additional 10-15 minutes until the cheese is melted and bubbly, and the edges are golden brown.
Garnish with chopped fresh parsley.
Serve the Lemon Ricotta Stuffed Shells with Spinach hot.

Enjoy this delightful and citrus-infused Lemon Ricotta Stuffed Shells with Spinach for a light and flavorful meal. Buon appetito!

Butternut Squash and Bacon Gnocchi

Ingredients:

- 1 pound (450g) gnocchi
- 1 small butternut squash, peeled, seeded, and diced
- 6 slices bacon, chopped
- 1 tablespoon olive oil
- 1 onion, finely chopped
- 2 cloves garlic, minced
- 1/2 teaspoon dried sage
- Salt and black pepper to taste
- 1/2 cup (120ml) chicken or vegetable broth
- 1/2 cup (120ml) heavy cream
- 1/2 cup (50g) grated Parmesan cheese
- Fresh parsley, chopped, for garnish

Instructions:

Cook the gnocchi according to the package instructions in a large pot of salted boiling water. Drain and set aside.
In a large skillet, cook the chopped bacon over medium heat until it becomes crispy. Remove the bacon from the skillet and set aside on a paper towel to drain.
In the same skillet, add olive oil. Add the diced butternut squash and cook until it's tender and slightly caramelized.
Add finely chopped onion to the skillet and sauté until it becomes translucent.
Add minced garlic and dried sage to the skillet, cooking for about 1-2 minutes until fragrant.
Season the mixture with salt and black pepper to taste.
Pour in the chicken or vegetable broth, stirring to deglaze the pan.
Add the heavy cream and grated Parmesan cheese. Stir until the sauce is smooth and creamy.
Add the cooked gnocchi to the skillet, tossing to coat the gnocchi in the butternut squash and bacon sauce.
Gently fold in the crispy bacon.
Adjust the seasoning if needed.
Garnish with chopped fresh parsley.
Serve the Butternut Squash and Bacon Gnocchi warm.

Enjoy this comforting and flavorful Butternut Squash and Bacon Gnocchi for a delicious autumn-inspired meal. Buon appetito!

Creamy Garlic Parmesan Spaghetti

Ingredients:

- 8 ounces (225g) spaghetti
- 2 tablespoons unsalted butter
- 4 cloves garlic, minced
- 1 cup (240ml) heavy cream
- 1 cup (100g) grated Parmesan cheese
- Salt and black pepper to taste
- Fresh parsley, chopped, for garnish

Instructions:

Cook the spaghetti according to the package instructions in a large pot of salted boiling water. Drain and set aside.
In a large skillet, melt unsalted butter over medium heat.
Add minced garlic to the skillet and sauté for about 1-2 minutes until fragrant.
Pour in the heavy cream, stirring to combine with the garlic.
Add grated Parmesan cheese to the skillet, stirring continuously until the cheese is melted and the sauce is smooth.
Season the sauce with salt and black pepper to taste.
Add the cooked spaghetti to the skillet, tossing to coat the pasta in the creamy garlic Parmesan sauce.
Adjust the seasoning if needed.
Garnish with chopped fresh parsley.
Serve the Creamy Garlic Parmesan Spaghetti immediately.

Enjoy this simple and decadent Creamy Garlic Parmesan Spaghetti for a quick and satisfying pasta dish. Buon appetito!

Shrimp and Avocado Pesto Linguine

Ingredients:

- 8 ounces (225g) linguine pasta
- 1 pound (450g) large shrimp, peeled and deveined
- Salt and black pepper to taste
- 2 tablespoons olive oil
- 3 cloves garlic, minced
- 1 cup cherry tomatoes, halved
- 1 ripe avocado, peeled, pitted, and diced
- 1/2 cup pine nuts, toasted
- 1 cup fresh basil leaves
- 1/2 cup (50g) grated Parmesan cheese
- 1/2 cup (120ml) extra-virgin olive oil
- Juice of 1 lemon
- Red pepper flakes (optional, for heat)
- Fresh parsley, chopped, for garnish

Instructions:

Cook the linguine pasta according to the package instructions in a large pot of salted boiling water. Drain and set aside.

Season the shrimp with salt and black pepper to taste.

In a large skillet, heat olive oil over medium-high heat. Add the seasoned shrimp and cook until they are pink and opaque. Remove the shrimp from the skillet and set aside.

In the same skillet, add minced garlic and sauté for about 1-2 minutes until fragrant.

In a food processor, combine cherry tomatoes, diced avocado, toasted pine nuts, fresh basil leaves, grated Parmesan cheese, extra-virgin olive oil, and lemon juice. Pulse the ingredients until you achieve a smooth pesto sauce.

Season the pesto with salt and red pepper flakes if you desire a bit of heat.

In a large mixing bowl, toss the cooked linguine pasta with the avocado pesto. Gently fold in the cooked shrimp and toss until the shrimp are well-coated in the pesto.

Adjust the seasoning if needed.

Garnish with chopped fresh parsley.

Serve the Shrimp and Avocado Pesto Linguine immediately.

Enjoy this refreshing and flavorful Shrimp and Avocado Pesto Linguine for a light and delicious pasta dish. Buon appetito!

Chicken Piccata with Angel Hair Pasta

Ingredients:

For the Chicken:

- 4 boneless, skinless chicken breasts
- Salt and black pepper to taste
- 1 cup all-purpose flour, for dredging
- 4 tablespoons unsalted butter
- 4 tablespoons olive oil
- 1/2 cup chicken broth
- 1/3 cup fresh lemon juice
- 1/4 cup capers, drained
- 1/4 cup fresh parsley, chopped

For the Angel Hair Pasta:

- 8 ounces (225g) angel hair pasta
- Salt for pasta water

Instructions:

Prepare the Chicken:

Season the chicken breasts with salt and black pepper.
Dredge each chicken breast in the flour, shaking off any excess.
In a large skillet, heat 2 tablespoons of butter and 2 tablespoons of olive oil over medium-high heat.
Add the chicken breasts to the skillet and cook for about 3-4 minutes per side until golden brown and cooked through. Transfer the cooked chicken to a plate and cover to keep warm.
In the same skillet, add the remaining 2 tablespoons of butter and 2 tablespoons of olive oil.
Pour in the chicken broth, fresh lemon juice, and capers. Bring the mixture to a simmer, scraping up any browned bits from the bottom of the pan.

Return the cooked chicken to the skillet and simmer for an additional 2-3 minutes, allowing the flavors to meld.
Stir in chopped fresh parsley.

Prepare the Angel Hair Pasta:

Cook the angel hair pasta according to the package instructions in a large pot of salted boiling water. Drain and set aside.
Serve the Chicken Piccata over the cooked angel hair pasta.
Spoon the sauce over the chicken and pasta.
Garnish with additional chopped fresh parsley.
Serve the Chicken Piccata with Angel Hair Pasta hot.

Enjoy this classic and savory Chicken Piccata with Angel Hair Pasta for a delicious and elegant meal. Buon appetito!

Sweet Potato and Sage Ravioli in Brown Butter Sauce

Ingredients:

- 1 pound (450g) sweet potato and sage ravioli
- 1/2 cup (115g) unsalted butter
- 1 tablespoon fresh sage leaves, chopped
- Salt and black pepper to taste
- Grated Parmesan cheese, for serving
- Toasted pine nuts, for garnish (optional)

Instructions:

Cook the sweet potato and sage ravioli according to the package instructions in a large pot of salted boiling water. Drain and set aside.

In a large skillet, melt the unsalted butter over medium heat.

Add the chopped fresh sage leaves to the skillet and cook until the butter begins to brown and the sage becomes crispy. Be careful not to burn the butter; it should have a nutty aroma.

Season the brown butter sauce with salt and black pepper to taste.

Add the cooked sweet potato and sage ravioli to the skillet, tossing gently to coat the pasta in the brown butter sauce.

Transfer the ravioli to serving plates.

Drizzle any remaining brown butter sauce over the top.

Garnish with grated Parmesan cheese and toasted pine nuts if desired.

Serve the Sweet Potato and Sage Ravioli in Brown Butter Sauce immediately.

Enjoy this delightful and comforting Sweet Potato and Sage Ravioli in Brown Butter Sauce for a tasty and elegant pasta dish. Buon appetito!